Keeping It Real

Margaret Jean Howard

Published in the United States of America

ISBN 979-8-89395-948-2 (SC)
ISBN 979-8-89395-946-8 (HC)
ISBN 979-8-89395-947-5 (Ebook)

Margaret Jean Howard
222 West 6th Street
Suite 400, San Pedro, CA, 90731
www.stellarliterary.com

Ordering Information and Rights Permission:

Quantity sales. Special discounts might be available on quantity purchases by corporations, associations, and others. For details, contact the publisher at the address above.

For Book Rights Adaptation and other Rights Permission. Call us at toll-free 1-888-945-8513 or send us an email at admin@stellarliterary.com.

This book is dedicated to my children, Angela and Robert, Jr, with my unconditional love.

Contents

Foreword

There is a time for everything, and a season for every activity under the sun (Ecclesiastes 3:1, NIV).

I am willing to tell the truth about my life and become vulnerable to all comments…, both positive and negative. It amazes me that multitudes of people have experienced things in life and refused to share their experiences with others. Others have accused me of saying too much about personal things. Those individuals who accused me of telling too much did not understand or take the time to get to know me well. To paraphrase a popular gospel song in the African American culture, if I can help somebody by sharing my life's journey through my writings, then my truthful sharing has not been in vain. My life has been full of surprises, some good and some bad. Today, I am grateful for the life God has given me. For too many years, I was not grateful for the difficult times, and I was even angry and disgusted at God for many years.

Because I've changed my heart over the years, I felt the need to commit and share some of my experiences on paper in the form of my second book.

This book is authentic and is not meant to tell anyone else's life except mine. This book includes some of my thoughts, feelings, decisions, and mistakes when those events occurred. They do not necessarily reflect my current thoughts and feelings or whether I would make those same decisions if those events were to occur now. I am so very thankful to God for numerous things. One of those things I am thankful to God for is that I do not have to relive my life a second time as it was. Yet, if I could, my heart's desire would be for God to give me my same beautiful baby girl who weighed six pounds and twelve ounces once I was happily married. To date, I do not understand why God chose me to endure the disgusting crime of rape at the age of eighteen and become an unwed mother. I believe other persons (female and male) who have endured heinous crimes feel the same as I do. Yet, I do not wish this heinous crime on any one just to spare me. God knew that I would be willing to share my life's journey openly and honestly with readers of my book. God had plenty of surprises just for me.

It would be very remiss of me to attempt to include all of my experiences of motherhood and family in this book. If I did attempt such a grand feat, I believe I would end up revealing personal situations that would result in embarrassment for others. My honest intentions were to be authentic at all times, to avoid including any material, although truthful, that would offend others rather than bless them, and to include only truthful scenarios involving my immediate family and myself primarily.

I've discovered that God does have a sense of humor, although many jokes people have told in my presence have been beyond my understanding. In those instances, I've relied on my husband, Robert, to explain those jokes to me. Some of them have been funny, and many of them have not. Either way, I am keeping it real.

Therefore, I tried to be as honest as possible when sharing the different aspects of my life, and hopefully, the readers will grasp the whole meaning of being very young and naive versus maturity and acquiring godly understanding and wisdom throughout my life's journey. Now, I know whole heartedly that I am stronger and more appreciative of the life God gave me. Glory to the only true living God!

Acknowledgments

I thank my daughter, Angela, and my son, Robert, Jr, for enriching my life in countless ways. Thank you, Robert, my husband, for falling in love with me at first glance. To my six grandchildren and two great-grandchildren, I thank you for helping me to relax, enjoy being loved, and enjoy each day to the fullest. I am very grateful to God for allowing me to republish my second book.

1
Why Me or Why Not Me?

The eyes of the Lord are in every place, keeping watch on the evil and the good. (Proverbs 15:3, ESV).

Oral history is very important to the African American tradition. Although the majority of white slave owners did everything humanly possible to destroy my enslaved Africans and African Americans ancestors' dignity and attempted to convince them that they were subhuman, lazy, ugly, ignorant, filthy, etc., my ancestors knew and remembered that they had had strong family ties and their homes were in mother Africa. My ancestors never chose to come to America. They were forced against their will. The mental and physical abuses my ancestors endured by the overseers bruised their bodies but not their souls. The overseers carried out the slave owners' harsh instructions.

As my oral history was passed down from one generation to another, Daddy urged all of his children to marry other African Americans because of the heinous sexual molestations and harsh beatings the girls and women we were descended from had suffered by the cruelty of their white slavers.

Grandma Mandy told Daddy that his grandmother had endured rape by the slave master while the slave master's wife waited in the big house…the home shared by herself and her husband. She gave birth to children fathered by the slave master and by her husband. My great-granddaddy had to wait out on his own front porch until the slave master finished raping his wife, and there was absolutely nothing he could do about it. Just imagine the pain and humiliation he and his wife suffered.

Nevertheless, my enslaved ancestors continued to think and believe what they thought. They continued the tradition of telling the families' history regularly. Grandma Mandy was responsible for telling our genealogy orally to her children. Grandma Mandy had thirteen children. Daddy was chosen to continue our oral tradition of telling our family genealogy, and Daddy passed this tremendous responsibility to my sister, Carrie.

My research revealed that the person responsible for remembering births, deaths, and marriages throughout the generations of the village was known as a griot. And not just anyone could be a griot. Traditionally, griots were men, although women have been griots. Being a griot was an honored position, not a position for just anyone. In an African village, the griot preserved their people's genealogies, historical narratives, and oral traditions since nothing was written down. The griots entertained the children through storytelling, and many of them were gifted with musical skills.

Daddy would frequently gather all my siblings and me around the fire in the evenings and tell us stories. He was a great storyteller; this was how we all learned our genealogies. Often, Daddy would open the large family Bible and show us the

Williams family's birth dates and marriage dates dating back to Grandpa Henry and Grandma Mandy. Information on Mama, Daddy, and all eighteen of his children was written in our family Bible. Daddy had the ability to remember a large amount of information.

Since I had the ability to memorize large amounts of information, unofficially, I thought I was the griot of the family after Daddy. I was sadly mistaken. Carrie knows much more than I do from memory. And now, I consult her whenever I need clarification about how different individuals are related to us. I've written down all of my family genealogies, including everything I knew about my paternal grandparents, parents, siblings, children, grandchildren, great-grandchildren, birthdates, marriages, etc.

From an early age, Daddy gave me the responsibility of keeping daily and weekly records of the field work production of each of our family members. I developed the habit of writing down important facts and details just because I had the tremendous task of keeping records of the money owed to us by the farmers. And I've continued this practiced throughout my lifetime.

During one of our annual Williams Family Reunion meetings many years ago, I suggested that we organize all of the branches of the Williams family and submit written genealogy on each branch, which would compile into one Williams' genealogical book dating back to our paternal grandparents, and this Williams' genealogical book would be updated as needed. Everyone was excited about my suggestion. This has been a terrific way to preserve our genealogies. Each branch of the Williams family has been requested to send updates on births, marriages, graduations, contact information, etc., to the family reunion committee.

As I have often traveled by car through small southern towns, the tiny unpainted houses appeared to be remnants of enslaved Africans' and African Americans' houses. They reminded me of the many houses Mama and Daddy rented during my seventeen years living in Alabama, the beautiful. Some of those old houses seemed to me to be unoccupied, but many had families residing in them. Some of those old houses were located quite a distance from the roads and streets, and others were located about the length of football fields or less from the roads and streets.

As a little girl, I remember the first house I lived in below Macedonia Baptist Church. It was unpainted, with a vast grassless front and backyard. The driveway was constructed out of large barrels covered with dirt and clay. When it rained, none of the dirt and clay ever washed away. It was as if a bull dozer had condensed the dirt and clay over those large barrels when the driveway was being constructed. The road in front of my house was unpaved, and it was normal to see bull dozers smoothing the roads.

Before I had turned six years old, Mama and Daddy moved my siblings and me into the second house I remembered. It seemed to be about half a mile off the main road. I did not mind the location of my house before I was school age, because my siblings and I played along that road often as we picked blackberries during the summer months. I was not aware of the possibility of any snakes lurking underneath the blackberry bushes at that time. If I had been aware of snakes, the chances would have been that I would have avoided all blackberry bushes regardless of how delicious those blackberries looked to me.

Before moving into the third rented house of my childhood, I entered the first grade, and it was then that half a mile became a challenge for a six-year-old girl every morning on her way to the school bus stop. My older siblings and I had to walk half a mile to catch the school bus, and if any of us were not waiting at the bus stop when the bus arrived, we would miss the bus and walk back home. I learned very quickly that I could not make it to the school bus stop on time if I did not leave myself plenty of time to walk that half a mile. Since I enjoyed attending school, I don't ever remember missing the school bus.

My parent's third rented house was located directly on a paved street. Since it was located outside a town or city, our home address was identified by a route number rather than a street address. It was the first house I had lived in to have neighbors within a couple of minutes' walking distance from my house. I enjoyed having playmates near my house, and the neighbors' children and I frequently played in each other's yards. If my memory serves me correctly, all of the houses my parents had rented up to this point had been unpainted. I had thoroughly enjoyed living close to neighbors, but my parents moved all of us into the fourth house of my childhood.

Although I dreaded having to move, my parents' fourth rented house was white-painted with electricity. That meant that Daddy and Mama did not have to burn kerosene lamps for light anymore, and my older sisters did not have to wash those delicate glass shades for those lamps. There was always a chance that either of my older sisters would drop one of the shades of glass lamps by mistake. I don't think either one of them ever did.

My parents' fourth rented house was located on a main unpaved road. Our nearest neighbors were located approximately equal distances east and west from us. We had very large front and backyards with a large tree in the front yard. This house had very large side yards with a large tree on the right-side of the house. The rooms were the largest rooms I had ever seen before in a house with black folks living in it.

I was overjoyed by the spacious rooms. Although there was a bedroom for the girls and one for the boys, the two double beds in each bedroom had spaces between the two beds in the middle and spaces on the outside of each bed. This was the first time I remembered having a dining room to eat all of our meals in and a huge kitchen with plenty of space for everything Mama needed in her kitchen. I don't ever remember being cramped for space when my siblings and I were inside my parents' fourth rented house. There were wall shelves in the dining room, which Mama used to store all the canned foods she prepared during those summer months. The younger children had plenty of space for the pallets to be placed on the kitchen floor to eat their meals, and the dining table was big enough to seat everyone else. I discovered that this house had been owned by white folks and lived in by the owner Daddy was sharecropping with. The owner had lived in this house for many years, had built a new house for himself and his family, and moved out of this one. Daddy was able to rent this house from him as soon as it became available.

When I discovered that my parents' fourth rented house was owned by a wealthy white land owner and farmer, it made sense to me why it was so spacious. All of the other houses my parents had previously rented were very small and had no electricity. Evidently, very few black folks were living in houses with electricity when I was seven-years old and living in the rural areas…outside of the town limits of Columbia, Alabama.

In the backyard, there were peach, fig, pear, and plum trees. Sometimes, my siblings and I would bite into the fruits growing on the trees too early and end up with very bitter tastes. We learned to wait patiently for all the fruits to ripen through our trials and errors.

As my siblings and I walked up and down the road we lived on, we discovered plenty of plum trees and blackberry bushes on both sides of that road. I discovered for the first time that there were blackberries and redberries to choose from. The red berries tasted just like blackberries. One of my older siblings warned me about the possibility of snakes being underneath the blackberry and redberry bushes. This was the first time I remembered being afraid to pick any blackberries and redberries in my life.

Going forward, I waited for my older siblings to pick the berries, hoping they would be willing to share some with me. I often walked along the roads admiring those delicious-looking berries, yet I was too afraid to pick any for myself.

During the years my parents lived in their fourth rented house, they decided to purchase their first television (TV) set. It came with antennas that looked like rabbit ears, and the TV was shaped like a large piece of furniture, which complemented the other furniture in the room. Having our own TV meant we did not have to walk to our neighbors to watch the TV shows.

I remember Daddy's favorite weekly TV show, Highway Patrol, starring Broderick Crawford. The entire family enjoyed that show. Yet, none of us spent our days watching TV. All of my free time was spent outside playing with my sisters until that fateful September when I was age seven.

My parents' fifth rented house was the same as house number one, two, and three had been. It looked as if it was a remnant of an enslaved African's or African American's house. It was unpainted, small, and located on an unpaved road. My parents, siblings, and I had neighbors a short distance from our new home, and Cassie and I frequently walked to their house to play with their children. They had two girls approximately our age.

To our surprise, Cassie and I discovered that these two new friends of ours would very rarely attend school, yet they attended church regularly. I did not understand why anyone chose not to attend school since attending school was the most enjoyable long-term endeavor I had ever experienced in Alabama, the beautiful state, for seventeen-years. I did not like living in my parents' fifth rented house at all. It was definitely too small for Mama's and Daddy's growing family, and we remained there for a few years. It was the last house Mama and Daddy rented while sharecropping, and they agreed that he would not ever again.

The sixth house Mama and Daddy rented was within walking distance of Columbia's city limit. Whenever I missed the school bus, I hurriedly walked the short distance to school and arrived there before the bell rang. That house was large, painted white, and had large rooms. I could tell from the history of my parents' fourth rented house that the owners had either previously lived in this one and/or it had been built for whites to live in. Again, I enjoyed living in my parent's sixth rented house because it was spacious, painted, had a large front yard, was located on a paved highway known as 95 East, and was no more than five minutes from a convenience store.

Although I thoroughly enjoyed living in my parents' sixth rented house, that was the first time I experienced significant hunger in my entire life because we did not live on a farm anymore. I had just taken for granted that there would always be enough food for all of us, although Mama and Daddy were still growing their family with more children. At that age, I was not aware of where babies came from. Usually, my free time was spent playing with my siblings and reading every book I could get my hands on. I was totally oblivious about where or how babies were born. As a matter of fact, I did not even think about any babies; I would just wake up one morning and have a new sister or brother. It was like magic and normal to me to have a new sister or brother in Mama's arms.

Henceforth, I was aware that there were many draw backs for my family and me, because we would never live on any more farms. All of our food would have to be bought, and Daddy was not a high-income earner. Therefore, all of the Williams' children who were old enough worked in the fields during the summer months for white farmers to supplement the family's income. Before, we would only work for pay for white farmers when we had caught up on the crops Daddy was responsible for. I continued keeping records of what each of my siblings and I earned daily and weekly.

After approximately one year of living in the spacious painted white house, Mama and Daddy moved us into a small, unpainted house across the street from my maternal grandmother, Big Mother. My parents' seventh rented house was located in the Town of Columbia, and my siblings and I walked to school every school day.

As I lived in Alabama, the beautiful from birth until age seventeen, it was apparent to me that the majority of black folks lived in substandard houses, whether those houses were rented or owned by the occupants.

Now, I don't claim to be an authority in life, I only know what has happened to me in my lifetime. I don't know the best way to raise children because each child is different. What works for one child does not mean it will work for another child. Each child has her/his own unique personality, and it is the responsibility of parents to learn each child's personality, appreciate each child's personality, encourage each child to appreciate her/his unique personality, and nurture the good in each child's personality. I know for a fact that I am not an authority on the ideal ways to raise children.

Yet, I do know that I am a person who can honestly share what has happened to me during my life's journey. I wear my feelings on my face, and I am thin-skinned. In other words, I don't hide my true feelings well and allow myself to be easily hurt. And I've never sought any retaliation toward others who have caused me pain and literally attempted to destroy me and my reputation.

From an early age, I was taught by my parents to guard my reputation at all times. I have been aware of my lack of defensive skills from a very young age when my sister, Cassie, would fight on my behalf and quickly respond to those persons who had spoken hurtful words to her and me. On the other hand, I remained silent as I tried to figure out what I should or should not do. I was never successful; I failed miserably every time, and Cassie continued to fight my battles physically. On many occasions, I asked Cassie how she responded quickly as I stood dumbfounded. Cassie would just shrug her shoulders and keep walking.

To date, I have never been involved in a physical fist fight and very seldom any verbal fights…if ever. Please don't misunderstand me. I can hold my own. The difference is that I am not impetuous when facing adversaries and making decisions, but rather, I choose my words very carefully in all disagreements and when making decisions. I know how a person feels when hurt because I have frequently lived with pain. And I disclaim the familiar rhyme that sticks, and stones may break my bones, but words will never hurt me. This saying is an absolute lie!

While researching this popular rhyme, I discovered it has been traced back to 1844 in a book by Alexander William Kinglake in London, England, as "golden sticks and stones." Later, it was cited in The Christian Recorder of March, published in 1862, stating that "sticks and stones can break my bones, but words will never hurt me." There have been various variations of this rhyme through the years. In 1872, it appeared in Mrs. George Cupples's piece, Tappy's Chicks, as: "Sticks and stones may break my bones/but words will never harm me."

Frequently, this rhyme has been used to defend against name-calling and verbal bullying, intended to increase resiliency, avoid physical retaliation, and remain calm and good-living. Well, sticks and stones definitely hurt someone physically, and that person eventually gets better and stronger after some time has passed.

However, the mental wounds from the popular rhyme stay for decades and keep burning in silence. The truth is that the power of words to deceive is a danger far exceeding any we might encounter from physical weapons. I know from my experiences.

However, I would rather be the person living with pain caused by others rather than be the one causing the pain. Oftentimes, I believed that if anyone could survive painful things and come out whole, healthy, and stronger, it would be me. My heart hurts for all people because I am my sisters' and brothers' keeper.

As a young girl, I remember dreaming every night. Oftentimes, I would dream about the naughty things I had done and forgotten away with, the offenses I had committed and punished for and the promises I had made to Mama and Daddy that I would behave and do better by thinking good thoughts. Mama and Daddy had told me numerous times that my actions initially originated as my thoughts. They urged me to think better thoughts and I would behave better. Other times, I would dream about how I wished my life would be and not how it was.

On the days I had misbehaved, I would not look forward to my bedtimes because I knew from past experiences that I would have nightmares while I slept. I would ask Cassie to hold my hand. She never refused, and she never questioned why I wanted her to hold my hand.

As I got older, I realized that my brain was continuously active with my thoughts. Every waking moment and every sleeping moment, I was thinking about something. Even when my mouth was closed, my brain was filled with thoughts. I must admit that some of my thoughts were not all good. Frequently, I would ask others what they were thinking about, and often, they said they weren't thinking of anything. Their answers always perplexed me, because I was always thinking about something. I wondered how a person could not think of anything. To date, I remain perplexed about their responses.

When I was a little girl, I heard many scary stories from different people, especially my older brothers. I was even afraid to be left alone in cemeteries because I thought some of the dead people's ghosts would appear and frighten me. I dreaded attending funerals even when I was in elementary school. But Mama and Daddy told me that I should attend my former fifth-grade teacher's funeral out of respect for her family.

To myself, I questioned why and how my non-attendance at her funeral would be disrespectful to her family. I had always shown Mrs. McLoyd, my former fifth-grade teacher, her husband, and her parents my highest respect. As a matter of fact, they had been neighbors of my family for many years, and I had played often with their children. My mind remained in a quandary, and I thoughtfully kept silent concerning that matter and obeyed Mama and Daddy by attending her funeral and homegoing celebration.

My dreams have motivated and inspired me to never give up on myself, even when things appear impossible. I constantly tried to think positively, not dwell on the negatives, and attempt to figure out the strategies I would need to accomplish my goals. The more I concentrated on positive things during my waking hours, the less I had nightmares. I remember that Mama and Daddy had encouraged me to think good thoughts because every one of my thoughts would become my actions.

After rededicating and recommitting my life to Jesus Christ, I would wake up early every morning and go walking before dawn. As a matter of fact, it was so dark that I could not see the ground or where I was placing my feet as I walked. By the time the sun had risen, I had been walking for at least twenty minutes. As I walked, I prayed to God, listened, and quoted Scriptures. My walks were mainly ninety minutes in length. I had a lot on my mind and needed a lot of time alone with God. I needed time with God to prepare me to face another day. God was the only one who thoroughly understood me.

All of my life, I have been criticized much more than I have been encouraged. I understood and accepted the fact that I needed the corrections offered by my parents, teachers, older relatives, and older siblings. And I understood and accepted responsibility for the errors I had made. But, most of the people who were quick to criticize me were usually those with very little or nothing positive going for themselves that I saw. Yet, those same people offered me advice supposedly for my own good, so they said. I kept quiet and wondered if they really believed their own advice to me.

For example, I was criticized numerous times for not physically fighting back. I was often criticized for not staying out after my curfew set by my parents, and I was criticized for not giving up my virginity as a young teenager. Some of the teenage boys went as far as to ask me what I was saving my virginity for, and they mean-spirited asked me if I was saving my virginity for the worms. Their responses hurt me tremendously. Mama and Daddy had taught me to remain a virgin until I got married. Even some of the fast girls attempted to pressure me into losing my virginity. Once I discovered they were fast, I stopped associating with those fast/loose girls in public, although we all attended church and school together.

My adolescent years were not fun and enjoyable but rather traumatic. I often wished to share my true feelings with Mama, but I was not comfortable enough, to be honest with her. You see, I did not want to hurt Mama's feelings. In addition, I was struggling and trying to keep my mind and thoughts pure. Yet, I did not understand how to keep my thoughts and mind pure because there was much evil in the world. I felt powerless against the prevailing evil.

On Sundays, the Sunday School teachers would emphasize that I should love everybody, even those who hate me and mistreat me. It seemed to me that plenty of people hated and mistreated me without taking the time to get to know me. I discovered at a very early age that my world was not color-blind. And hate was exhibited toward me by black, brown, and white folks even as I was growing up in Alabama, the beautiful. In addition, I discovered that it did not take any effort to hate oneself and people, but it takes much effort to love oneself and others.

If I were to concentrate on the things, I was displeased about myself, then my mind would remain on my dislikes more than on the things I liked about myself. It perplexed me that black and brown folks were of the opinion that people with narrow noses, straight hair, and light skin were naturally more beautiful than people with wider noses, curly hair, and dark skin. And, of course, I had a broad nose, curly hair, and brown skin.

This popular belief of numerous people continued to perplex me, so I asked God for clarification in this matter because God created all of us. I asked God directly if God made narrow-nosed, straight-haired, light-skinned people naturally more beautiful than those who were not. I never received an answer directly from God to my question and remained perplexed. I remember hearing some Sunday School teachers and some preachers say God is a just and fair God, and I thought to myself that if God promoted discrimination of any kind, then I would not embrace a God who discriminated against anyone.

I learned Old and New Testament Bible verses as a child and attended Sunday School every Sunday. The Old Testament Bible verses such as Deuteronomy 14:2 brought me no comfort, no assurance, no confidence or self-esteem. Deuteronomy 14:2 says for you are a holy people to the Lord, and the Lord has chosen you to be a people for His own possession out of all the peoples who are on the face of the earth. I did not embrace this Scripture because I was not a Jew, and my family history dated back to being Christians and not Jews.

In my study and research over the years, I've located at least one hundred Scriptures about God's chosen people, since growing up in Alabama, the beautiful, and more than thirty have been located in the Old Testament.

Because those people in power in Alabama, the beautiful did not look like me, and those with no power in their daily lives in Alabama, the beautiful looked like me, I did not automatically feel good about myself. So, I had to work very hard to convince myself that I was beautiful at the beginning of elementary school. Very early in elementary school, I noticed that most of my teachers primarily asked light-skinned girls and boys to erase the black board and pass out the graded papers.

I wondered to myself why black folks chose to continue living in Alabama, the beautiful, and why black folks ever chose to move to Alabama, the beautiful. According to documented history, many slave owners moved to Alabama, the beautiful in search of cheap and productive land on which to grow cotton. Most of these slave owners came from nearby states such as North Carolina, South Carolina, and Georgia. I have not found any reliable information on black folks who willingly moved to Alabama, the beautiful, during the time I was growing up there.

As I searched and read books about black folks, I never came across any blacks who had chosen to settle down in Alabama, the beautiful. However, the noteworthy black folks in the books and articles I read had settled in Massachusetts. None of them had been borne there, and I began to focus on moving to Massachusetts in the future.

Therefore, I surmised that the majority of Africans and African Americans had been brought to Alabama by their slave owners and not of their own choosing. According to my research, twenty to thirty enslaved Africans landed in Virginia in 1619 at Point Comfort, known today as Fort Monroe in Hampton, Virginia. The year 1619 marked the beginning of race-based bondage that defined the African American experience in the United States.

In addition, I wondered why Alabama was known as Alabama, the beautiful. Maybe Alabama, the beautiful was used as its slogan in order to attract only more white folks because my experiences of living there at that time discouraged blacks from relocating there due to the actively enforced Jim and Jane Crow laws and the non-inclusive attitudes of black, brown, and white folks.

To comfort myself, I practiced writing down the characteristics that described me and constantly repeated those characteristics to myself. I would stand in front of the mirror and repeat my characteristics with a positive spin to myself as I smiled at my reflection in the mirror. I said, "My high forehead held my big brain; my broad nose enhanced my keen sense of smell, and my dark skin shined like the dawn of the sun."

I made much effort to stop concentrating on my characteristics as being ugly, but rather, all of my characteristics were beautiful in the sight of a loving God and not of a discriminatory God, because a loving God never made any mistakes. I repeated the following Scripture repeatedly that says God created me in God's own image, in the image of God God created man; male and female God created them (Genesis 1:27, NIV, paraphrased). I was included in that Scripture…God's Word.

Although I was raised in my home church from a very young infant, baptized as an infant, baptized a second time as a preadolescent, and confirmed, I struggled with the Bible verses that said God's chosen people. The environment I was living in daily did not clarify God's true meaning of those words, and no one seemed to be able to explain God's words so that I understood them. I believe that many preachers lacked some of God's wisdom and understanding, just as many adult believers lacked some. I wished they would have been bold enough to admit to me that they just did not know the answers to my questions and advised me to pray to God for the answers, to trust and depend on God for clarity as they prayed for me, and answers. At least I admitted to myself that I did not understand many things written in the Bible as a child, and I still don't understand them as an older adult, although I am an ordained minister in the American Baptist Churches.

When I was in the sixth grade, I competed in a school spelling bee. I was an excellent speller and received perfect grades on my spelling quizzes because I practiced a lot. Yet, I forgot how to spell the word separate during the spelling bee. I was very disappointed because I honestly believed I would represent my sixth grade in the state-sponsored spelling bee. And I was knocked out of the competition because I forgot how to spell the simple word separate. I had difficulty believing what had happened, because I knew how to spell that word and had a memory freeze. Actually, this is the first time I have shared this incident publicly. I told God all about how disappointed I was in my spelling efforts and decided that I would study and practice more. I never entered another spelling bee. So, at the age of twelve, I realized that spelling from memory was one of my weaker skills. I had already discovered that writing was one of my weaker skills earlier in elementary school.

By the age of fourteen, I had visualized and dreamed over and over again about the way I desired my life to be once I was independent of Mama and Daddy. I knew it would take many years of hard work, commitment, and determination to rise above my current life and lifestyle. I had imagined myself as a doctor wearing a white lab coat with a stethoscope around my neck and talking to patients. I had seen myself dressing for work with beautiful clothes and comfortable, stylish shoes to choose from. I had seen myself living in a beautiful, well-furnished, air-conditioned house.

At the age of fourteen, I experienced Black History month nine times, which was always the entire month of February. Every one of my teachers emphasized to me to learn my history…black folks' history, and not rely on the textbooks being used in the segregated schools. Since all of my teachers had attended historically black colleges and universities (HBCUs), they were very knowledgeable in black history. My teachers had read extensively and listened to the oral histories told to them by their college professors, their relatives, and many others.

As I listened to my teachers' presentations during each Black History month, I began reading as much as I could on successful black folks beyond Booker T. Washington and George Washington Carver. I admired Sojourner Truth and Harriet Tubman immensely. I had much difficulty visualizing myself accomplishing anything in the magnitude of Harriet Tubman, because I had a severe phobia of snakes and many other wild animals. I could not imagine myself traveling long distances in the woods to rescue enslaved Africans and African Americans. I was not brave enough. It has been documented that Harriet Tubman, known as Black Moses, made at least thirteen trips to Maryland through the underground railroad and led at least seventy enslaved people to freedom. I believe she successfully completed numerous more trips freeing enslaved Africans and African Americans.

But I could imagine I would accomplish something similar to what Sojourner Truth had done since she had been an outspoken advocate for abolition, temperance, and civil and women's rights. I visualized myself as a successful doctor committed to worthy causes in my communities. I thought if God had made a way out of no way for Harriet Tubman and Sojourner Truth during the industrialized enslavement of black folks, the same God would make way for me to accomplish my educational goals without a doubt.

My thoughts, imaginations, and dreams were all opposites of my current life. Mama and Daddy would have to call my name several times before I would answer them, because I was lost in my thoughts about my future. Both of them would remind me to stop daydreaming and get to work. I obeyed them and continued to imagine my future. The fantastic thing about my thoughts, imaginations, and dreams was that I could resume them all at the point I had been interrupted. I believed this was a special gift I had, and I kept silent about this special gift.

Now, in hindsight, God knew all of my insecurities. God knew all about my trials and tribulations. God knew all about my hurts, pains, and disappointments. God even knew all about my doubts. As a matter of fact, God knew me better than I knew myself.

Once I had recommitted and rededicated my life to Jesus Christ, I just took the time to unload everything on God each morning, even if it meant being sleep-deprived, and I was sleep-deprived for many years. If I had not taken time to be alone with God each morning, I know I would not have been able to function as well as I did. I knew God was in me, with me, and went before me. And whatever happened each day, God had prepared me to act, do, and think. By the end of each day, my usual words were "thank God." Then, I would depart for home.

About ten years ago, a nephew said, "The only way I could live with being raped was because I believed in God." Before responding to his comments, I thought for a moment. At that time, he was still struggling with an addiction, but this time, he was depending on God for strength and not on his own strength to overcome his addiction. After a few moments had past, I said, "You are absolutely correct." And I told him I was holding on to God's unchanging hands, even if I developed callouses.

During my teenage years and adulthood, I wished I had a mentor to help me navigate life's challenges. There have been many individuals who have been willing to help me do wrong and make wrong decisions. Still, very few individuals have been supportive and encouraging, and even fewer individuals have helped me develop self-esteem and confidence. Oftentimes, I stood before the mirror in the bathroom, encouraging myself and smiling as I talked to myself. Many years ago, I made up my mind that I would not do unto others as they had done unto me, but I would do just the opposite…do unto others as I wanted them to do unto me! It wasn't easy.

The first person who had taken a personal interest in me beyond the responsibilities and duties of her profession was the school librarian, my seventh-grade English teacher, Mrs. Hines. I consider her my first and only true mentor while growing up in Alabama, the beautiful because my whole world was expanded due to her interest in what I read daily in the library during my lunchtimes. I began to expand my imagination into areas I had never imagined before, and I began to imagine that I would be able to accomplish things that there was no concrete evidence to support my new ways of thinking. I was twelve years old in the seventh grade.

At that time in the seventh grade, the word mentor was not part of my vocabulary, and besides, Mrs. Hines, no adult of much consequence ever came forward to help me maneuver through the many obstacles I would face in the future. If they did, I was totally unaware of any. I believe that if anyone had reached out to me, I would have recognized them, because I have never exhibited any attitudes that would cause me to reject help from genuine people.

As I stated before, several individuals have accused me of telling too much about my circumstances and personal experiences than I should. When I did this, it was me crying out for help. It was my way of letting others know that I cared enough about them, that I was willing to be vulnerable, and that I would share some of my deepest hurts and disappointments with them as a witness so that they would overcome their problems just as I had done.

Once, I was attending Forsyth School for Dental Hygienists; I discovered that all of my white classmates were very familiar with the word mentor because they had had mentors since they were in middle school. They had been guided and encouraged to identify professionals they would like to shadow by the time they were in the ninth grade. My classmates told me that their mentors had been instrumental in setting up interviews with professionals for them to shadow.

Well, I was already at more of a disadvantage in more ways than I had realized as far back as the eighth grade. Even at the age of fourteen, when I had decided that I would become a doctor, there was not a black or brown doctor in my hometown of Columbia, Alabama...no medical or dental. If I had known what the word mentor meant, I would have been too intimidated even to approach the only doctor in Columbia, because he was white.

With the exception of one of my white classmates in hygiene school, all of them were eighteen and nineteen years old. I was twenty-five, and the older white dental hygiene student was at least a year younger than me.

Without being mentored on a continuous basis, it had taken me eight years to enter a two-year college program rather than two years as I had planned. Even then, I was not attending a four-year college. One of my dental hygiene instructors advised me on the process of getting admitted to Northeastern University after graduating from Forsyth.

Yet, it would please me very much if I could recall having at least one successful mentor who was constantly there for me during the most painful times in my life. But there was not even one successful person in my corner. God even provided one ram for Abraham so that he would not sacrifice Isaac. It would not be until I became a dental medicine doctor that God provided me with the best mentor, I could ever have…The Rev. Dr. Michael Wayne Walker.

As I am writing this book, the COVID-19 pandemic is in its second year, and the dominant variant is omicron. Although I have been fully vaccinated and had my booster shot, I continue to practice those mitigations recommended by reputable public health experts, because I love myself and simultaneously love others. There have been multiple millions of people who have died from COVID-19. Some have died from lack of knowledge, fear, misinformation, lack of access to the vaccine, etc. I've listened and continued to listen, and most of all, I pray to God for guidance in making good decisions. God has never failed me yet!

My brain does not comprehend the mentality of some people. I was watching the news (CNN or CBC) about a thirty-one-year-old husband, father of two with another child on the way, who was in intensive care on a ventilator needing a heart transplant. He had been on the top of the list for a heart transplant until he had refused to be vaccinated against COVID-19. As a result, he lost his priority on the heart transplant list, and the opportunity passed to the next patient who had been vaccinated.

When the COVID-19 vaccine was being developed, I, too, had said there was no way I would be taking a vaccine that had not been tested on people for at least ten years. I had taken my first flu shot only after it had been tested on people for a minimum of ten years. Besides, I actually don't trust the government to act in my best interest, because I remember reading about the Tuskegee Study of Untreated Syphilis in the Negro Male. The study had 399 men with syphilis and 201 without the disease. This study began in 1932.

Even after it had been proven that the antibiotic penicillin was the drug of choice, 399 black men were not treated with penicillin. The United States Public Health Service committed a crime against humanity and should have been held accountable. According to my research, those 399 black men had been misled with a blatant lie. And that blatant lie was that they were being treated for bad blood. The only compensations those 399 black men received were free medical exams, free meals, and burial insurance.

I faced this dilemma in early 2020 when the COVID-19 vaccine was being developed. God had already helped me with my decision before the end of 2020, because I had fervently prayed to God for instructions and guidance about the developing COVID-19 vaccine. When Pfizer announced that older patients were included in their trials, I knew God had answered my prayers.

Initially, Pfizer had included patients much younger than I was, and I knew my immune system was not the same as when I was fifty years old. I could have scheduled my COVID-19 vaccination with the front-line workers, which meant that I could have had my vaccine administered to me in December 2020 and early January 2021, depending on appointment availability.

Since I was retired, I waited until President Biden opened the COVID-19 vaccination to all people sixty-years and older. I did not need to take up an appointment earlier than February 8, 2021, because I was not in the presence of COVID-19 as the frontline workers were. My action concerning the COVID-19 vaccination was merely my way of demonstrating that I love and care about all of God's people since I am my sisters' and brothers' keepers.

On February 14, 2020, I took a trip to Plain, Georgia, on Valentine's Day weekend. I wore a face mask while I was at Boston Logan International Airport and on the plane as I traveled to Atlanta, Georgia. And I had done the same on my return trip.

On March 3, 2020, I attended Sunday School at Messiah Baptist (MBC). As the class was nearing its end, I stated that we needed to stop all handshaking, stop sitting close together, and ensure we frequently handwash with soap and water, because there is a contagious, deadly coronavirus in the environment. Also, use hand sanitizer when soap and water aren't available. Although there had been some push back, I had already stopped my double-hugging much earlier. I was not known for handshaking anyway because I had been a germophobe since dental school. So far, I have not had any form of COVID-19. Thank and praise God!

By the way, I believe people some of the time, and I believe God all of the time, although I only have a partial vision of what God's world should be and only a partial understanding of God's written Word (referencing First Corinthians 13:12, NIV).

I honestly believe that as I continue to draw near to God on a regular basis in prayer, meditation, reading the Bible, and quiet time, the most important aspects of my life will become evident to the readers without me specifically mentioning them by name. And by me asking God those tough questions, God will reveal more eternal truths and answers to my tough questions.

During the COVID-19 pandemic, I have had plenty of time to muse over the most important things to me. I am not rushing through life. Although my brain remains as active as when I was very young, I am taking the time to thank God for waking me up every morning and enjoying every day to the fullest, because tomorrow is not promised to me.

As you read this book, some of the most important things to me will become evident to the readers without me mentioning them by name. Here goes!

2
Ready or Not

See to it that no one takes you captive by philosophy and empty deceit, according to human tradition, according to the elemental spirits of the world, and not according to Christ (Colossians 2:8, ESV).

The primary difference between being poor in America as a child today and being poor in America in the era I was born in was that I grew up in a two-parent household. Don't get me wrong. There have been multitudes of single parents who have raised their children with much success. And they still do. The fact was that the majority of children in my hometown lived in two-parent households. In those few circumstances, with only one parent in a household, grandparents were usually there to help raise the children. I knew that when I arrived home each day, Mama would be there, and Daddy would come home from work every night. It never entered my mind to think or believe otherwise for the first seventeen years of my life.

A secondary difference between being poor in America as a child today and being poor in America in the era I was borne was that the fathers were not incarcerated. There could have been instances where some of them were jailed for minor offenses for a short time. If so, I was never aware of any. The other fathers of children worked at different low-paying jobs, just like Daddy, and many of them also worked at more than one job.

On weekends, it was well-known that some of the fathers would congregate and drink moon shine. It was unusual for them to drink their moon shine in the presence of children. Some of the children knew their fathers had been drinking because the fathers would arrive home intoxicated or tipsy. I never witnessed my father drinking any alcoholic beverages, intoxicated, or tipsy, although some of my older siblings have told me they do. Evidently, that phase of Daddy's life occurred before I was borne, or I was too young to recognize whether Daddy had been drinking.

The majority of parents were the pillars of our community. They were our role models, and it was common practice for them to model the behavior they desired of us…their children. I am not attempting to portray all parents as being perfect individuals, because I am sure they all sinned and fell short of the glory of God. Nevertheless, the adult parents acted like responsible adults in the presence of the children. It was common practice that those responsible adults knew they had the right to reprimand all misbehaving children verbally. They knew when the children should be in their own yards. Children in elementary and middle schools would all be in their own yards before sunset.

As a matter of fact, the responsible adults believed that they all had the right to question all children they felt were disobeying their parents when the parents were not around. I remember that, on many occasions, the adults urged me to hurry home before Mama or Daddy caught me not being in my own yard before the sun went down.

While I lived in Alabama, the beautiful as a child, I was aware that black folks and white folks were treated differently by white folks. But, I was never fearful of being harmed by any black folks or white folks. Usually, I did not just wake up in the mornings thinking about white folks. I woke up every morning thinking about things that pertained directly to my family, community, and me.

Although I knew I would not remain in Alabama, the beautiful any longer than I had, I never experienced any fear as I walked along the roads and streets. My desire to leave Alabama, the beautiful was attributed to the limited opportunities available to me. My family and I were poor not because Daddy was lazy but because he had limitations placed on him when he was a child and throughout his adult life.

Mama and Daddy were very wise. They were very spiritual and full of God's wisdom and understanding. They embraced God's principles literally and raised all of their eighteen children according to Proverbs 13:24. Proverbs 13:24 says parents who spare the rod hate their children, but the ones who love their children is careful to discipline them (NIV).

A tertiary difference between being poor in America as a child today and being poor in America in the era I was borne was that usually, on Sundays, everyone attended church…entire families. There were always more children in Sunday School and worship services than adults because most parents had large families, especially those who were farmers and used to farm. As a matter of fact, I knew very few children who were not from large families.

There was no excuse for any of the children not knowing proper behavior because we were taught proper behavior in the homes; we were taught proper behavior in Sunday School, and we were taught proper behavior in school. I grew up when all of my Sunday School teachers were African Americans, all of my pastors were African Americans, and all of my school teachers were African Americans, also. My world did not involve interacting with white folks in my personal and social existence. White folks were there, yet they were not on my mind when I woke up in the mornings; they did not occupy my thoughts during the day, and they did not occupy my thoughts in the evenings. My life existed separately from the white folks.

When I was fourteen, I became aware of the grave disparities that existed between being black and being white, and this was the time my thoughts began to be about white folks occasionally. This was about the time that I could arrive home a little later than after the sun went down. I could not remain away from home alone at age fourteen, but I could be away from home with schoolmates and girlfriends a little later. I could attend birthday parties and school dances with friends at age fourteen as long as I was home by 9:00pm.

Because Mama and Daddy had given me more freedom, my eyes were opened to the fact that there were limitations on the activities a fourteen-year-old could do. Learning to swim in swimming pools was not allowed because of the whites-only signs. Sitting down in restaurants with my friends and ordering whatever I desired was prohibited because of the whites-only signs. Going to the public library to read and check out books was not allowed because of the whites-only signs. Sitting down at the counters in the drug stores to order ice cream and soda was not allowed because of the whites-only signs.

It was as if I had been living with blinders over my eyes until I turned fourteen. At the age of fourteen, I was beginning to see and experience the injustices in the world for myself and not from my parents' and other adults' experiences. Up to the age of fourteen, I had been under the watchful eyes of my parents and the entire village. I had lived within the boundaries of the village, and I had not considered doing otherwise.

At age fourteen, I could leave the house and go out and about with my girlfriends. My girlfriends and I would walk to each other's houses and proceed with whatever we had planned without any accompanying adults. I began to notice that most of the white teenage girls and boys were riding in cars; most of them went swimming in the local swimming pools, and girls wore beautiful clothes regardless of what season it was. I noticed that the white girls and boys could sit at the counters, order whatever they wanted, and sit in restaurants and dine in. I did not like anything I witnessed, and I kept quiet and did not verbalize my distaste and disgust.

Although I had been taught that God loved everyone the same, I wondered why white folks had better access, more opportunities, and a better quality of life than black folks in Alabama, the beautiful. Mama and Daddy said it's not God; it's because those white folks did not know any better. Then, I would ask them why white folks did not know any better. And Mama and Daddy said, "Because they chose not to know better." I wondered why God allowed the white folks to treat black folks that way since God was mightier than everyone.

Being old enough to leave my parents' home without their permission and simultaneously not being disobedient to them was something I was eagerly looking forward to. I wholeheartedly believed I would make it on my own and succeed through hard work and dedication.

It seemed that the next three years would never pass. And it was impossible for me not to notice the things that I lacked, such as beautiful clothes and the freedom to enjoy all the activities that the white girls my age had opportunities to enjoy. As a matter of fact, I felt that God was not providing me with all the things I needed and none of the things I just wanted. Yet, I continued to attend Sunday School and worship services every Sunday. Attending Sunday School and worship services was something Mama and Daddy taught me. It was our family tradition. And so, I prepared myself to be there every Sunday. Besides, I enjoyed being in Sunday School and worship services with my friends.

When I was in the eleventh grade, two of my classmates became pregnant and were not permitted to continue attending school. I thought to myself that this was unfair because the boys who made my two classmates pregnant were allowed to continue attending school. They experienced no repercussions from becoming fathers. I discovered that even black folks were guilty of discriminating against their own folks. Before my classmates were permitted to reenter school, they had to apologize to the school committee before being allowed to resume their education. The teenage fathers never had to do this, and they were free to continue making more babies without any repercussions, if they chose to.

During some of my discussions with Daddy, I would ask him difficult questions, and it was during one of those occasions Daddy told me that he was one of the parents who had advocated on my classmates' behalf to be allowed to continue their education at the high school. I had already made up my mind that I would not anticipate marriage until I was at least in medical school, so having a serious relationship with a boy during my teenage years was out of the question. Only fast girls had premarital sex.

At least that was what my parents had taught me, and since I was not fast, I would remain a virgin. This was not difficult to do because I chose not to have a boyfriend. In this way, I was spared the pressure of a boyfriend to move a relationship to another level. I made sure that all my friendships with boys remained platonic in nature.

Although I was still single, I became pregnant at the age of eighteen, less than a year after arriving in Massachusetts, and I was still not a fast girl. I was raped and became pregnant as a result of that rape. Regardless of the heinous crime I endured, I was still pregnant and unmarried. All I had going for myself was a high school diploma. And economically, my high school diploma did not translate into my ability to earn a living wage. It was already very challenging living on my own in a big city. But being poor, pregnant, single, and uneducated in a big city was a tragedy. Although I was a young adult at the age of eighteen, I was totally unprepared to become a mother, and I felt trapped against my will. Why God? Why did you allow me to be raped? I was in grave despair.

Since suicide was never an option for me, because I believed that I would end up condemned (in hell) throughout all eternity if I killed myself. Therefore, I prayed to God to allow me to sleep into eternity. Yet, God woke me every morning, and I was disgusted and angry at God. First, I was angry at God for allowing the rape to occur, and second, I was angry at God for not answering my nightly prayers in the way I had prayed. I was forced to figure out what I had to do on my own. Where was God when I needed God? God was nowhere to be found as far as I was concerned. I did not feel the presence of God! God had failed me, I believed!

One would think that I could return home to my parents in Alabama, the beautiful. But, for me, this was never an option. I had escaped from there and was determined never to live there again. Also, I felt that I could not endure the shame of being pregnant and unwed. I was not strong enough to bear the harsh and mean-spirited gossip of folks who had known me all of my life. I believed they would want to think the worst of me and say I had turned out to be fast.

I was beginning to understand what Mama and Daddy meant when they said, “If I make my bed hard, I would have to lie in it, and a hard head makes a soft behind.” Well, it took me three months to realize that God was not answering my prayers the way I desired. Therefore, I decided to make the best out of my horrible predicament. Absolutely nothing was turning out the way I had imagined and dreamed.

For several years, I had imagined and dreamed about the way my life would be once I moved to Boston, Massachusetts. I thought I had to work hard and live the way Mama and Daddy had taught me daily. Once in college, I would study hard and consistently, forego college parties, and not get involved with boys until I graduate and enter medical school. I was very naïve by anyone's standard in so many ways.

Maybe, I stood out like a country hick…out of place. Yet, I did not feel out of place in Boston, Massachusetts, because Boston represented higher learning; it was where everybody who wanted to attend college could and where older students were accepted and welcomed. I knew I would be one of the older students, because it would take me at least two years to prepare for college. So, I thought.

Because Mama and Daddy were strict disciplinarians, I had made several attempts when I was under their authority to figure out what I could get away with and what I could not. I knew I could sometimes fool them, but I could never fool God. Therefore, I feared Mama and Daddy more than I feared God, because Mama and Daddy had long memories. They would remember my mistakes and little lies for days, weeks, months, and years.

Since I had been taught by Mama and Daddy that God was loving and forgiving and Jesus Christ had died on the cross for all of my present and future sins, I believed the only thing God would not forgive me was suicide. So, I decided to concentrate on growing a healthy baby…ready or not!

I could write that I was very happy with my unwanted pregnancy. If I did that, it would be a complete lie! It was very difficult for me to think of one thing that I was truly thankful for during my first pregnancy, because I still did not want to be pregnant, nor did I want to give birth to a baby. I desired only to have the responsibility of taking care of myself. I had never been a free loader. Since I learned to work ten hours in the brutally hot and humid weather beginning at the age of seven during the summer months, I was determined never to become a free loader at age eighteen.

However, I frequently indulged in my private pity parties, and it has taken me several decades to cease hosting them. During my first pregnancy, I held frequent pity parties just for myself until my baby was borne. I can honestly say that I never remembered enjoying being pregnant. I just endured it. I got through it the best I knew how. At the age of eighteen, there were plenty of things I did not know and had not lived long enough to be taught. I told my growing baby everything while I carried her in my womb. I emphasized to my baby that she and I were blameless. And at that time, I placed all blame on the rapist and God! Actually, I blamed God more than the rapist, because God could have struck that man dead before he committed the heinous crime of rape.

Nevertheless, my baby and I would get through this pregnancy together. I could have benefitted from merely an ounce of Mama's and Daddy's wisdom, because I knew I was lacking in many areas. During my pregnancy, I remember working long hours, taking frequent walks, frequently talking to my baby as I explained everything to her, singing to my baby, and frequently reading happy books. I was very lonely and sad most of the time and seldom laughed. I missed the sounds and feelings of laughter, but under my current circumstances, there were few things to enjoy and laugh about. I ceased praying to God in the mornings and at night before bed.

Although my earning potential remained limited, I took advantage of the local free libraries located throughout the neighborhoods. All of them were conveniently located on or near bus routes, and a few were within walking distance of my different apartments. The luxury of free libraries was a novelty to me, because I had not had the privilege of checking out books from libraries for seventeen years of my life, except my school library. If any free public libraries were in existence in Alabama, the beautiful they were limited to white folks.

For the first time in my life, I had unlimited access to public libraries, and all I needed was a library card. It was almost too good to be true. I applied for my library card as soon I discovered they existed and continued the practice of maintaining a current one. My joy of reading continued without interfering with my current income, and I made sure that I never incurred any late fee charges.

The job I had during my pregnancy was just another factory one. All I did was sit at a machine and attach colored lights to electrical cords. It did not require any training to learn this job; it was very mundane and tedious. I earned enough money to support myself and save a little weekly until the birth of my baby.

However, I had to figure out what I would do about my living expenses once I had given birth until I could return to work. The medical doctor at Boston City Hospital told me that a postnatal examination was required after giving birth to my baby. I learned that when I stopped working and when I would return to work, it was known as maternity leave, but I had not earned any paid maternity leave from my factory job, because my job did not offer any employee benefits. I estimated that it would be at least twelve weeks before I could begin working again, including the time it would take me to gain employment.

Therefore, I applied for welfare, which went against my values. But this was the only option available to me since I needed time to recover from childbirth. Up until the time I wrote my first book, Robert, my husband, was the only person who knew I had been on welfare for a few months. Having to resort to depending on a biweekly welfare check from welfare was very embarrassing. Therefore, I never discussed the matter with others.

Since I have experienced non-consensual sexual intercourse and unwanted pregnancy, I have frequently pondered why some parents continued to become pregnant casually without thinking things through, especially women and girls. Only women and girls carry growing babies in their wombs; they personally experience every symptom associated with pregnancies, and they are the ones who undergo all of the agonies of childbirth. Then, there are the long periods of recovery after each birth, losing excess weight, and sleep deprivation for numerous months. Some fathers experience their fair share of sleep deprivation, as they rightfully should.

I had wondered if any of those rapists ever considered the grave harm they caused when they raped nonconsenting females. I have wondered if those rapists would reap what they sowed while they were alive as the result of them raping females. And I wondered if the rapist who raped me would ever become remorseful for his action and ask God for forgiveness before he died. I do know that the rapist never asked me for forgiveness.

In addition, I have wondered how those rapists could live their lives as if they had never committed any sexual crimes against women and girls. I have wondered if any of those rapists ever married and fathered any girls. I believe there have been millions of girls and women who had been raped just as I had been and bore similar pains and sufferings, humiliations, unworthiness, uncleanliness, inferiority complexes, and all other negative feelings and emotions as I had.

While going through my first pregnancy, I decided she would be an only child. I decided that I alone would have total control over my body, although adoption remained an option for me, if I desired more children in the future after marriage. I knew that I had enough love in my heart to love all children, and I did not need to experience another personal pregnancy.

Finally, a six-pound twelve-ounce baby was borne, and I was committed to providing all the love and attention she so deserved. Financially, I could not afford to give her a lot of material things. However, my baby was never deprived of her mother's love…my love. My love and attention were free and freely given. I named my baby, Angela; she was God's gift to me. I loved her unconditionally.

All the feelings of lack of love and attention I had been deprived of during my eighteen years were showered on Angela. I remembered that I never had been hugged and kissed enough by my parents. I had often felt that Mama and Daddy had been unfair in their treatment of me. I often felt that Mama and Daddy had placed too much responsibility on me. The housework, field work, and helping with the care of my younger sibling were very demanding on my time. If I failed to carry out any of my assigned chores, I would experience their displeasure, because Mama and Daddy had long memories.

When Angela was borne, I was not qualified for a higher-paying job, because I lacked the necessary skills they required.

Yet, I was done with all factory jobs. Therefore, I went to various employment agencies and inquired about office positions. The only office job I was qualified for was a file clerk, and I applied for a position at Kemper Insurance Company located at 260 Tremont Street, Boston, Massachusetts. I was hired on the same day and started working there soon afterward. My sister, Arola, was Angela's childcare provider and lived less than one block from me.

Each day, I rode a bus and subway to and from work. I was used to starting my days early each morning because of my ten years of fieldwork experience. Therefore, I was never late arriving at Kemper Insurance Company each day. Whenever overtime was offered, I readily worked the extra hours. I needed the money. I notified the welfare office and told them I had acquired a job at Kemper Insurance Company as a file clerk. The social worker attempted to talk me out of starting to work so soon after giving birth. I assured her that my doctor had cleared me for work. The social worker informed me that I would receive a few more checks before closing my files. If my memory serves me correctly, I received at least two more welfare checks and definitely not more than three.

When Angela was six months old, Nellie, a younger sister, came to stay with me to care for Angela during the summer months. This gave Arola a much-needed break from her childcare obligations. I promised Nellie new school clothes as payment for her caring for Angela that summer. Nellie took care of Angela very well, and I was very pleased with our arrangement.

Nearing the end of that summer, I went shopping for school clothes for Nellie and was very surprised at the cost of everything. I ended up in Filene's Basement. Unfortunately, I failed Nellie miserably when purchasing her new school clothes. I just could not afford the type of clothes she wanted. I regretted this terribly.

About six months after Nellie returned to Alabama, the beautiful, Arola and I moved to Jamaica Plain together, and an older woman who lived across the street from us became Angela's childcare provider. It was during the first year Arola and I shared an apartment that I met my future husband, Robert.

Angela was a happy baby and toddler. I worried that my state of mind while carrying her in my womb would affect her negatively in some way. I even discussed my concerns with her pediatrician. He assured me that Angela was very healthy and was thriving in all areas of the childhood development indicators. I made sure that I spent as much time as possible with Angela when I was not working. I took her to the park and on walks. I read daily to her and sat on the floor, teaching her how to talk. I made sure that the library books and the few books and toys I had purchased her were utilized regularly. I enjoyed reading to Angela as I showed her the pictures in her books. She often fell asleep in my arms as we sat on the floor or in a chair. Bedtime stories were integral to our nightly routine when I did not work overtime.

Eventually, Angela refused to go to sleep without me reading her two and sometimes three stories. Of course, I always chose a short third story to read to her on those occasions. I took advantage of the convenient locations of the various free public libraries throughout the community and regularly checked out children's books to read to Angela and some strictly for my enjoyment. I avoided checking out any horror books for myself. But, I readily read every other genre of books.

In hindsight, none of those books I read to Angela on a regular basis included any Biblical stories or Bible verses. I don't recall saying a prayer with Angela as I tucked her into bed. I had separated myself from God, although God never separated God's self from me.

I don't proclaim to be an authority in raising a child. As a matter of fact, I am far from it. It's just that this was the hand I was dealt, as one would say, and I was doing the best I could under the circumstances. In the back of my mind, I would always ask myself what was the correct way to do this or that. Or simply, what should I do in this situation? I actually had no confidence in my ability to care for an infant. I was unsure if I had fed Angela correctly and whether I was burping her the right way. When it was time for diaper changing, I was unsure of the entire process. I was concerned about rubbing her delicate skin too harshly and making sure all of her feces had been removed. So, I relied on my sense of smell, which never failed me.

In hindsight, I know God was helping me. But, at that time, no one could convince me that God was guiding me in raising Angela. I don't recall ever saying or feeling glad to be an unwed mother. Although I loved Angela with all my heart, as a devoted mother, I could forever love her child, and I still do.

Being a file clerk allowed me to earn extra money and attend a business school at night, located a few blocks from Kemper Insurance Company and on Tremont Street. Between the older childcare provider and Arola, I was never concerned about Angela. Both of them went beyond the call of duty and were very reliable. I never had to call out sick because Arola and the other provider took care of Angela, even when she was ill. I had no worries or concerns when Angela was in their care.

After about six months as a file clerk, I was promoted to a code clerk, which meant a little more money. I could continue to work overtime each week and attend business school at night. By the way, I attended two different business schools, and the fastest I ever learned to type was thirty words per minute. This was with me looking at the keys as I typed. Eventually, this light typing skill would help me obtain a better job years later. But, at that time, it did not benefit me financially.

For a couple of years, Angela was my whole world. Everything I did was for her. I was determined that she would never regret that I was her mother and never feel wrong about her conception. When I thought about the Virgin Mary, she was only fourteen and unmarried when she became pregnant with Jesus. I never gave my consent to the rapist. Yet, both of us ended up pregnant and unwed mothers. For Mary, it was an honor to be the mother of Jesus. For me, it was complete shame, dishonor, and disgrace. Yet, Angela was without fault and loved by me no matter what, and my daughter inherited only good genes from me. I rejected all references of the rapist regarding the purity of my daughter because that sexual perpetrator was dead as far as I was concerned. And if he was not, I hoped he was in hell (condemned) on earth and in hell forever in eternity.

Once Robert and I married, Angela's last name became Howard, and there were no more blank spaces on her birth certificate. There was never an ideal time to tell Angela about her genealogy, and time waits for no one.

I signed her up for ballet when Angela was three years old, which did not last. Then, I signed her up for piano lessons, and the same thing happened again. Once Angela was in first grade, she chose to learn to play the flute, which lasted a little longer than the other arts. As it turned out, Angela was not proficient in any of those endeavors and showed little interest in them. I wanted Angela to become competent in the various performing arts, but Angela was not interested.

However, Angela took to swimming by age seven and was never tired of being in the water. It was obvious that Angela enjoyed swimming and was very good at it. I had a rude awakening during the time Angela became very competent in swimming. I remember promising myself that if I ever had a daughter, I would make sure she had dancing, swimming, and piano lessons beginning at a very young age. She would have all of the things that I had not had, which were in part due to lack of money on my parents' part, and the rest was due to the discriminating Jim and Jane Crow laws. Now, I had exposed Angela to many of my unfulfilled desires, and she chose only swimming. It is true that a person cannot live another person's life. I learned to sit back and enjoy that Angela enjoyed swimming and did not have to worry about the cost.

I was older and married for over five years when Robert Jr was born. I was not concerned about paying the bills anymore and all the other things that had been paramount on my mind during my first pregnancy, because Robert was an integral part of our lives. I felt very secure in my personal life after I was married. I felt less vulnerable to insults and what others thought. There were some people who would always believe the worst and place blame on the wronged individuals. Once I was married, I had Robert to protect the both of us from physical harm and the vicious gossip of others.

Since Robert Jr was born with my consent, there was no embarrassment and shame associated with my second pregnancy. I had acquired parenting skills and confidence in feeding, burping, diaper changing, bathing, etc. Yet, I would call the pediatrician every time Robert Jr ran a fever. I did this until the pediatrician kindly told me to give him liquid Tylenol every four hours and intermittently take Robert Jr's temperature. Then, call him back, if Robert Jr's fever persisted. Well, I only had to be instructed to do this once. Henceforth, I was confident the majority of the time as to whether I should notify Robert Jr's pediatrician or not.

Angela was walking at eleven months, and Robert Jr was walking at nine months. Angela was speaking clearly and in training pants well before she was two years old. Robert Jr took his own good time learning to speak clearly and wore diapers much longer. Both children were healthy and learned to do things at different ages. This was not a problem or concern for me, because I knew never to compare my children and just be aware of their development.

Another thing I remember about Angela and Robert Jr. was that they were totally different. Whereas Angela enjoyed playing alone as long as she could see me, Robert Jr enjoyed playing in and out of my sight. With Robert Jr, I often had to search for him once he crawled and walked. Usually, I found him playing in the toilet or the kitchen. Angela was very easy to please. She adapted well to the naps, storytimes, baths, and bedtime routines. Angela's bedtime gradually changed as she got older.

On the other hand, Robert Jr did not adjust well to any of those routines. At three months, Robert Jr refused to take naps when I scheduled them and would profusely cry when it was his bedtime. I was so distraught with his behavior that I made an appointment with his pediatrician about his behavior. I actually thought that something was very wrong with my son at the age of three months, and I was very concerned. The pediatrician asked me, "What was the latest time I could tolerate Robert Jr remaining awake each night." I quickly replied at 9:00pm.

Therefore, 9:00pm became Robert Jr's bedtime at the age of three months and remained so until he was in the eighth grade. As a matter of fact, Angela never made an issue about Robert Jr's bedtime being much later than her bedtime every night. She enjoyed being read to and reading to herself once she had learned to read, and Angela had numerous books to choose from once Robert and I were married.

3
My Children's Formative Years

No discipline seems pleasant at the time, but painful. Later on, however, it produces a harvest of righteousness and peace for those who have been trained by it (Hebrews 12:11, NIV).

After surviving the heinous crime of rape, in hindsight, I wish I had had an intimate and personal relationship with God during my pregnancy. The truth was that I was very far away from God. I existed every day purposely, not trying to concentrate on being obedient to God or desiring an intimate and personal relationship with God. Now, I am not proud of this fact. It is just the truth, and it would be well into Angela's teenage years before she discovered that I was attempting to live my life to please God.

As it turned out, my daughter was born when I was nineteen, and my son was born when I was twenty-six. The main difference between my two pregnancies was that the first birth was not my choice, and the second one was. I have heard parents say that their sons were much easier to raise and nurture than their daughters, especially during their adolescent and teenage years.

For me, I was anxious most of the time when both of my children were very young, especially when they could not talk, and I had to figure out what they needed and when they needed things. I felt much more comfortable as my children grew older and developed their personalities. I even encouraged them to express themselves honestly, speak up, and not be shy. I did not want them to believe that children should be seen and not heard. I wanted them to know that they had the right to be seen and heard by me.

I can earnestly say that raising a daughter and son presented many challenges, and I just tried to be the best mother possible through it all.

As long as I was in the room, Angela played with her dolls as if they were real people and true friends and engaged them in conversations. She even read them stories once she had learned to read. Usually, I never needed to stop doing my chores or studying when Angela entertained herself during her formative years. I worked full-time and attended night school part-time during Angela's formative years.

Regarding Robert Jr., he could not care less about me being in the room with him. I was working full-time and attending college full-time during Robert Jr.'s formative years, except for the nine-and-a-half months he was developing in my womb during my last year of dental hygiene school. He was hyperactive as long as he was awake. His pediatrician advised me to just keep him busy during the day. Robert Jr enjoyed taking his toys apart and putting them together again. Oftentimes, he failed miserably in his attempts to put his toys back into their original forms. But this did not deter him one bit.

I felt so ill-equipped and immature when Angela was born for such a tremendous responsibility of being a good mother. I felt just the opposite when Robert Jr was born. During my adolescent years in Alabama, the beautiful, I never totally desired to be a mother, and if I would ever become a mother, I would be happily married and a doctor first. Never in my wildest dreams and imaginations had I visualized that I would be an unwed mother first; I would get married second, and third, I would have a second child. To make matters more difficult, I was pregnant with my son during my second year of dental hygiene school at Forsyth School for Dental Hygienists in Boston, Massachusetts, although it was my choice to become pregnant.

I was determined to do things much better than my parents had done for me. In hindsight, Mama and Daddy instilled much more in me than money could buy. Mama and Daddy taught me to love God, myself, and others. Mama and Daddy taught me to pray to God early in the morning and at night before going to sleep; Mama and Daddy taught me to treat others the way I wanted others to treat me, and Mama and Daddy taught me to depend on God and trust God for everything. Unfortunately, I did not actively attempt to depend on God and trust God when raising Angela.

During that period of my life, I believed that God did not love me and care about me enough, because God had allowed me to be raped, and to make matters worse, God had allowed me to become pregnant as a result of being raped. Therefore, I did not want anything to do with a God that would allow such a heinous crime to happen to an eighteen-year-old teenager who was just trying to get ahead in life. I was working hard and attending business school at night. I was enjoying life with my sister, Cassie, and the few friends we had met. None of us were street-wise, and we were about having some good, clean fun.

Since I was raised in a church from an infant, I had continued this tradition by joining Grant African Methodist Episcopal Church and regularly attending it every Sunday. So, I questioned the God who had put me in such a horrible predicament…raped, pregnant and unwed. How was I to feel the love of God? How was I to depend and trust a God who had deserted me in my time of need? All of those Sunday School lessons and memorized Scriptures did not enter my mind to help me through this heartbreaking and traumatic experience.

If only I had remembered Proverbs 3:5-6, which says trust in the Lord with all my heart and lean not on my own understanding; in all my ways acknowledge God, and God will make my paths straight (NIV, personalized). Ecclesiastes 10:2 says the heart of the wise inclines to the right, but the heart of a fool to the left (NIV). After the rape, I leaned on my own understanding, and my heart inclined to the left, and I did not realize that my decision to do this was a grave mistake. So, I went on with my life as a backslider and did not have a guilty conscious, because I blamed the rapist and God for my life being turned upside down.

So, I went on with my life in my own strength and understanding, determined to be a much better parent to Angela than my parents had been to me.

During the first couple of years, after Angela was born, I took her to my friend Diane's church for a while. Angela would attend children's church while I attended the traditional worship service every Sunday. Angela had plenty of attention and fun in the children's church and hated to leave there on

Sundays. I could not blame her because there were many children to play with, and just the two of us were at home. As a matter of fact, I was still taking Angela to church on Sundays when I met my future husband. Yet, I did not develop a close relationship with God and was not aware that I needed one.

As I was committed to being the best mom possible, I read to Angela and Robert Jr at night before bed. Sesame Street was their favorite TV program, and I took advantage of that time to complete other tasks I had on my schedule. I had very little time for myself during Angela's and Robert Jr's formative years. I was always pressed for time. I was always on the go. I tried my best not to let them know I was pressed for time.

The weekly cleaning, washing, grocery shopping, and cooking were completed before I took them outside to play or to the zoo and/or to a movie. Most of the time, I fell asleep during each movie and would wake up just when the movie was ending. Angela and Robert Jr. never interrupted me as I slept, because I had taken them to the bathroom before entering the theatre and provided plenty of food and beverages to enjoy as they watched the movies. The three of us went to the same Walt Disney movies several times, and neither complained about seeing the same movies repeatedly. This pleased me very much.

I learned that Angela and Robert Jr had no concept of my time with them. But they remembered how often I was with them. So, throughout their formative years, I made frequency of time a priority. This helped me tremendously to manage my time to study for exams and all the other chores I had to complete. Again, I had imagined that I would have a maid/housekeeper by the time I would be a mother, which was another misconception of my reality.

For many years, I desired a housekeeper, but Robert would not agree to one. When Angela and Robert Jr. were very young, I managed to keep the house clean because every night before bed, I would pick up things off the floor, freshen up the bathrooms, wash the dishes, etc. Their messes were easy for me to handle. As they got older, their messes became overwhelming. I was the only neat person of the four of us. Therefore, the children followed what their daddy did. They became a slob right along with him without any shame. The older they became, the messier they were, and my need for a housekeeper magnified.

Finally, it dawned on me that I did not need Robert's permission to employ a housekeeper. I had a job; I wrote out all the monthly bills and was responsible for keeping our home in order. It would be wonderful if I could say that Robert was a great help with the housework, grocery shopping, etc. But that would be a great big lie. Occasionally, Robert did help with different chores, and whenever he did, he wanted me to thank him. Can you believe that? This was an insult to me. At first, with a smile on my face, I just said, "Thank you, Robert, for folding the towels or whatever." Then, I just stopped thanking him because he had used the towels just as I had, and he never thanked me for doing the weekly laundry. The nerve of him!

I did not consider Robert's lack of engagement in routinely doing our family chores worthy of frequent arguments. I just functioned as if I were a superwoman for many years, and it was very exhausting. Whenever I had a chance on the weekend, I would read a book and fall asleep in the afternoons. If Robert and I had any social commitments, naps were essential for me to stay awake. Otherwise, I would be yawning by 9:00pm.

The age gap between Angela and Robert Jr became very noticeable when Angela was in middle school. As a preadolescent, Angela desired to be with children her own age and enjoy ice skating in the winter and roller-skating year-round with them. I did not blame her at all for not wanting her little brother tagging along with her and her friends.

I must admit, Robert Jr was very curious about Angela's room, as he used to wander off and play in the bathroom, toilet, and kitchen once he learned to crawl and pull himself up. He was always destroying Angela's completed schoolwork and moving her things around to his liking. I felt very bad for Angela as she agonized over the situation. I held her very close to me as I attempted to explain that she used to make messes throughout the house, and I would patiently clean up the messes. Now, it was her turn to be patient with her younger brother. Eventually, he would learn to stay out of her room and only enter it with permission.

As I remember, Angela scolded her brother regularly and cried many tears before Robert Jr grew old enough to understand his actions thoroughly and stopped going into her room without permission.

During this period of time, I took Angela and Robert Jr with me to Sunday worship services. I never attended Sunday School and did not consistently attend the same church on Sundays. I purposely chose to visit different churches so that I would remain inconspicuous. By the way, I sometimes missed attending church on Sundays. When I attended worship services, I hoped Angela and Robert Jr would become familiar with Jesus and Jesus' love for them, not the God who had failed me. Proverbs 22:6 says to train up a child in the way she/he should go: and when she/he is old, she/he will not depart from it (NKJV, paraphrased).

Although I did not desire them to know the God who had deserted me, I was torn, and I was living every day in a spiritual war and did not realize it until many years later.

As Angela adjusted to having a nosy and active brother, I was sure she complained to her friends about her brother being a constant pest. Angela loved to laugh and be with her friends. One of her friends was bilingual, and she taught Angela French. Another one of her friends taught her Spanish. Speaking other languages was easy for Angela because she could roll her tongue. To this day, I still cannot roll my tongue. Yet, Angela was a natural, and once she was speaking French and Spanish, Angela began to learn conversational Portuguese and Italian.

Angela attended private schools from preschool until the second grade while we lived in metropolitan Boston. Actually, Angela attended the same parochial school in the first and second grades. Once we moved to Brockton, Massachusetts, Angela attended public school until she graduated from the eighth grade. On the other hand, Robert Jr attended private schools from preschool through kindergarten and public school from the first grade through eighth grade. Robert and I chose parochial schools for Angela and private schools for Robert, Jr in hopes that both of them would learn more about Jesus and Jesus' love for them.

The City of Brockton only had one large high school, and I had no confidence in the Brockton Public Schools teaching black and brown children at the high school. Some older parents of children being educated at Brockton High School shared many of their disappointments with me, especially the disparities in educational opportunities their children suffered at Brockton High School. Therefore, Robert and I enrolled Angela in a parochial school from the ninth grade onward, and she thrived and was very successful there.

When Robert Jr was in the second grade, the four of us moved to Easton, Massachusetts. Angela continued at the same parochial school, and Robert Jr continued in the second grade at Easton Center Public School.

Since Angela and Robert Jr. have been living their lives independently of Robert and me, they have shared numerous rules of ours that they disobeyed while they were living with us. First of all, when they first told me of their adventures, I was just thankful that I had not experienced the numerous hours of worries and concerns they would have caused Robert and me if we had known about their prior adventures as they were occurring. Those unsupervised adventures began when Angela was thirteen or fourteen, and Robert Jr was six or seven while we resided in Brockton, Massachusetts.

Since Angela was older than Robert Jr, he had no choice but to go along with what Angela said, and I honestly believe he never objected to going on those adventures. According to them, they would take the shortcut to the Westgate Mall. This shortcut was a well-used trail through the woods, which ended at Westgate Mall. Angela said they took the wooded trail so that they would not be seen by people in the neighborhood who may have known us. Neither one of them ever considered there could have been pedophiles, murderers, kidnappers, thieves, and bullies lurking in those woods. They were just concentrating on getting to the mall as fast as possible, enjoying their time with friends, and returning home before Robert or I arrived home.

After Angela and Robert Jr told me about their unsupervised adventures to the Westgate Mall beginning at ages thirteen or fourteen and six or seven, I asked them how they would feel if their children sneaked to a mall through a wooded trail at the same ages they were at the time. Both of them appeared startled by my question and at the thought. Both of them felt that the times had changed drastically for the worse since their childhood. I told them dangers existed when they were children, just as dangers exist now.

Well, I reminded them that pedophiles, murderers, kidnappers, thieves, and bullies have been committing heinous crimes for thousands of years. And by the way, the first murder was committed during Biblical times by a brother killing his own brother...a familial murder.

I never thought either one of my children had been saints or had always followed Robert and my rules. Still, I was surprised that they had been bold enough to venture to the Westgate Mall at such young ages without parental permission or a trusted older person, especially when neither of us was in Brockton during those adventures. As the saying goes, children will be children.

4
Relying on My Upbringing

Children are a gift from the Lord; they are a reward from him (Psalm 127:3, NLT).

With my full and demanding schedule, I managed to graduate from Forsyth School of Dental Hygiene on time. I had completed my last year of a two-year dental hygiene program, having been pregnant since October of the previous year, and I was scheduled to give birth to my second child on June 17th. As it turned out, my baby was very comfortable in my womb and chose to be a week late. I had gained forty-four pounds and was very uncomfortable. I just wanted my baby out of me. I could no longer sleep in a bed at night. I slept in one of the recliner chairs in the living room because I could adjust the back.

Every time I attempted to sleep, my baby would become very active and would not stop kicking until I got up and walked around for a few minutes. I told myself that I was rocking my baby back to sleep.

Because I had experienced pregnancy sickness the majority of the time during my second pregnancy, I was not able to tolerate many healthy foods, although junk foods such as ice cream, cookies, and doughnuts were well tolerated. Therefore, my selections of healthy and nourishing foods were the same each day and limited. I had acquired a terrible eating habit that would take me years to overcome.

Angela was swimming as if she was related to a fish when Robert Jr was born, and Robert Jr. was swimming very well by age four. I never had to worry about them because they were very skillful swimmers. As for me, I have always been an awkward swimmer because I did not take swimming lessons until after the birth of Robert, Jr., And by that time, I had developed a phobia of deep water.

I used the same principles with my two children that I practiced for myself. I taught them to believe that if they worked hard and remained honest, they would succeed in any endeavor. I encouraged and praised them constantly; I congratulated them whenever they persevered through difficult tasks they had undertaken, and I taught them that they only failed when they stopped trying.

I always felt that I did not receive enough hugs and kisses from my parents, and I could have benefitted from more frequent praises and encouraging words from them. I only remember receiving praise and encouragement from Daddy. This memory does not bring me pleasure; acknowledging this to myself is just a fact. Yet, the truth remains that I don't recall Mama ever telling me that she was proud of me for anything. With all the house chores I had to perform, and the time I spent caring for my younger siblings, Mama never praised or thanked me. I've always wondered why.

During the first seventeen years of my life, there were numerous conversations I wanted to have with my parents, but I never had the nerve to approach certain subjects. I was afraid to discuss my displeasure with Mama. I was afraid to express my displeasure of Mama with Daddy because I knew it was something Daddy would not tolerate. I've always attempted to avoid confrontational situations all my life. As long as everyone remained calm, I was willing to be part of the discussions. Otherwise, I remained quiet.

Therefore, I allowed Angela and Robert Jr to ask as many questions as necessary until they understood. They often told me I was being old-fashioned or outdated in my opinions and rules. In many instances, I pulled rank on them and said, "I am their mother, and what I said stands." They did not like me saying this, but they could do nothing about it.

On many occasions, I emphasized to both that God would hold me responsible for raising them the way I was doing, and God would judge me and not them. I told them, in the meantime, to learn to be obedient and do a better job raising their own children than I did in raising them when they became parents. I did not force either of my children to talk to me when they were upset with me, because I had to engage in numerous conversations with Mama and Daddy when I was angry with them. I knew to give them their own space.

As a matter of fact, I was immensely relieved that they did not want to talk to me or be in my presence, because I felt the same way toward them. My priority was to be the best mother I could be, and I did not have any supporting evidence to guide me except my conscience.

Frequently, many parents are concerned about being friends with their children rather than focusing on being the best parents, because all children are gifts from God and deserve good parents. I have never prioritized being friends with my children, grandchildren, and great-grandchildren. If being their friend interfered with me being a responsible parent, grandparent, and great-grandparent, then I did what I thought best. Everyone knows friends come and go, but a mother, grandmother, and great-grandmother remain who they are even through tough relationships!

Mama and Daddy were committed to raising their children so that they would be upright and productive in life. They desired that we had a relationship with God and modeled the behaviors they believed would be good examples for all eighteen of us. It has taken me several decades to understand Mama and Daddy more. They did not purposely overlook or neglect me. It was just that their plates had been full of parenting responsibilities twenty-four hours every day, and they did the best they could under those circumstances.

Oftentimes, I saw and listened to Daddy on his knees praying to God very early in the mornings, and many times, it sounded as if he was crying or near crying. I continued quietly listening until I heard Daddy mention my name. Then, I would stop listening and leave. I never stayed around to hear Daddy say Amen. In hindsight, Angela and Robert Jr never heard me pray fervently to God the first ten years of their lives. And I grew up hearing Mama and Daddy praying to God from a very young age. I don't even remember not hearing them pray in the mornings.

A mother, grandmother, and great-grandmother don't stop being who they are. Parents, grandmothers, and great-grandmothers need to remember this fact. Someone should maintain a sound mind through it all. Trends come and go. But true parenting, even through tough times, lasts lifetimes.

Although I was never involved in physical fights, my two children were. I consistently taught and modeled the behavior of settling everything with diplomacy, which was achieved through conversations as each party actively listened. Diplomacy and peacemaking were two of my stronger skills; I've had many years of practice utilizing these skills, and I actually believed that these skills needed to be taught to my children.

Well, Robert had other ideas. He taught them that if anyone laid their hands on them, they should hit back as hard as possible to teach those offenders a good lesson they would never forget. Neither one of my children listened to my advice on how to handle conflicts. They followed their daddy's advice about how to handle themselves during conflicts and were very proud of themselves. So, I left all of the phone calls from the school administration for Robert to respond to, except for one of Angela's many school offenses.

I personally handled this one particular school offense, because I discovered that Angela had written several notes and forged my signature on each one. The headmistress at Angela's school informed me that Angela had been excused from school on several occasions by presenting those excused notes from me. I went to the school and informed the headmistress that I never wrote or signed any of those notes. I pleaded with her to only give an in-school suspension for Angela's offenses.

Otherwise, Angela could have viewed a school suspension as a reward. The headmistress agreed to my request. As Angela and I were in the car, I stopped on the side of the street after we were a couple of blocks from her school; I slapped her face and instructed her to get in the back seat and cry as loud as she liked, then I continued to drive her home.

Once home, I told Angela to go directly to her room and choose the dress she would be buried in, because I was going to send her home to her Maker. Then, I called Robert and told him the entire scenario and asked him to come home immediately before I murdered our daughter. Robert rushed home. I was in our bedroom lying down when he arrived. Robert quickly went to Angela's room and had a long conversation with her. They talked for quite some time. I did not ask any questions. I was fed up with Angela's behavior and relinquished all further serious and in-depth discussions to Robert. I had reached my wits' end. I only knew how to pray to God to guide Robert and Angela.

As Angela spent every school day in the library during her week-long in-school suspension, I continued to be perplexed about her behavior. As it turned out, Angela and her friends had been playing hooky from school for several days and had driven to Cape Cod on those days. This was Angela's senior year of high school, and she never thought that her behavior could or would disrupt her future plans, such as attending her senior prom, her high school graduation, entering college in the fall, etc.

While pondering Angela's actions, I thought that Angela did not appreciate how fortunate she was. As I was comparing Angela's opportunities to attend schools well-equipped with everything with my lack of opportunities when I was growing up in Alabama, the beautiful, I was very angry with Angela. I did not have any words to explain my anger and displeasure adequately. I thought that if I had what Angela was taking for granted when I was growing up, I would have become a doctor in my mid-twenties rather than in my early thirties. I was very perplexed about the whole situation.

Besides, I had looked forward to attending school every day, and I had to miss an entire month of school each year from the time I was seven years old until I graduated from high school at age seventeen. I explained to Angela that Robert and I had made sure that she and Robert Jr would never have to experience the hardships we had as children. Angela knew that from the age of seven, I had to pick cotton for the entire month of September, which meant I was a month behind the other students attending school from the second through the twelfth grade.

Angela was playing hooky from school with a few of her girlfriends to spend the day at the beach in Cape Cod. I thought I had raised an ungrateful child who did not know how fortunate she was. I thought that from the time Angela was three months old in my womb, she was paramount in all of my decisions. I had worked very hard to make sure she would never be ashamed of me for being her mother. I began to wonder if Angela valued her life or if she subconsciously wanted to fail.

From the age of eight, Angela stated that she was going to be an attorney. I thought to myself that because of the way she was going, she might as well forget about law school, because Angela may not make it into college, if she did not graduate from high school. I did not know what the parents of the other offenders thought, but playing hooky was a serious offense to me. How else could a person acquire an education except by attending school, participating in classes, turning in assignments on time, and successfully passing all quizzes and examinations? I reasoned that Angela could not successfully complete those tasks, if she played hooky.

I had been aware that other parents had experienced problems with some of their children, but it never occurred to me that my own daughter would have the nerve or thought to behave in the manner that she had. Angela knew how much I valued and appreciated acquiring a good education. And she had observed me working and attending different educational programs for as long as she could remember. I had been attempting to better myself in life. And I had often informed Angela that it did not matter where I started. But what mattered was where I ended up. I had emphasized to Angela that I was only a failure when I stopped trying and gave in to defeat.

Once Angela had turned sixteen, she and I frequently disagreed. I felt as if my daughter had switched places with another sixteen-year-old teenager. Angela's attitudes and personality were utterly foreign to me. I constantly asked Angela if everything was alright with her or if there was something I could help her with. She never opened up to me about what was bothering her. I was concerned but didn't know what to do about it.

Angela would say, "I hate you." And I would say, "No, you don't; you just think you do." My responses would anger Angela even more. You see, I understood Angela's feelings toward me at her age, because I felt that I hated both of my parents at the age of sixteen. However, the difference between my parents and me was that I had given Angela permission to ask me all the questions she desired, because I never wanted her to be afraid and uncomfortable with me about anything. Yet, Angela never whole-heartedly confided in me until she was in her twenties.

One would think a child would be very grateful to have parents who were involved and encouraged her to do her best in-school and her personal hygiene. And the only regular house chore Angela was responsible for was keeping her room clean. Although Angela was supposed to wash and iron her own clothes in the eighth grade, I regularly completed her washing for her because I said to myself that I was doing laundry anyway.

As I attempted to figure out what and how to interact with Angela, Robert and I suggested that Angela talk with a therapist. Angela agreed, and I began walking in D.W. Fields Park every morning at 5:00 am.

On the other hand, in Angela's eyes, her daddy could do no wrong. Even when he scolded her, she listened and apologized to him. But, for me, it was just the opposite. Oftentimes, I sent Angela to her room and waited for Robert to address the situation, and I retired to my bedroom for peace and quiet. From age sixteen until twenty-one, Angela did not like how I talked, walked, dressed, looked, etc. I knew it was only a phase she was going through, but I was perplexed about how long it would last.

For five years, I did the majority of my parenting of Angela through Robert. I did such things as taking Angela shopping for clothes and shoes and to her doctor appointments. Robert practically did all of the recreational things. He would drive Angela to the basketball and football games. Angela would locate her friends at each game and go off. Robert wouldn't see her, until after each game had ended, and it was time to leave and drive home. Sometimes, I dropped Angela off at the ice and roller-skating rinks.

Throughout these challenges of nurturing Angela through her adolescence and teenage years, I was very grateful to Robert, because he maintained an excellent parental relationship with Angela. I never heard her tell her daddy that she hated him. Somehow, Robert always got Angela's cooperation in keeping her promises to him. This resulted in Angela acquiring her license as soon as she was sixteen and a half and driving her own car the next day.

Angela never discovered that the things she and her daddy talked about were the things Robert and I had discussed privately. Robert and I had plans A, B, and C for each situation. If plan A did not work, plan B was implemented. If plan B did not work, we implemented plan C, which was starting the process all over again to come up with new plans A and B. Plan C actually meant that plans A and B were not working. We needed to start our private brainstorming discussions about Angela all over again to formulate new plans A and B.

Those years were very turbulent and painful for me. Yet, I endured them as best as I knew how. I remembered what goes around comes around. It was my payback time. Except for one thing: I had never had the nerve to talk back at either of my parents. I had to mind my manners and show respect toward my parents, which meant I had to behave as if my lips were sealed with super glue, although my thoughts were not. However, once, I attempted to talk back at Mama when I was fifteen-years-old and found myself on the kitchen floor as if a lightning bolt struck me on the cheek and knocked me to the floor. From that one experience, I knew not ever to attempt to be fresh with Mama again. Some children don't learn from one experience. I was not one of those children.

During this period in my life, I discovered the need to recommit and rededicate my life to Jesus Christ, because I had begun to experience inner loneliness within my innermost being. I also began to go to the gym twice a day. I arrived at the gym every morning before it opened and walked inside with the person opening up the gym. Then, I went to the gym every night to relieve the day's stress and prepare myself for possible trouble at home. I was relieved and thankful on those infrequent nights when no problems needed my immediate attention. It was amazing to me that I did not develop hypertension or tachycardia due to the tremendous stress while Angela was still at home and behaving as she was.

While exercising on the treadmill in the mornings, I would read the Bible, and in the evenings, I meditated on Scriptures I had memorized. I developed a habit of memorizing and personalizing long passages of the Scriptures. This helped me to live each day in a state of prayer with God's thoughts so that God would guide my thoughts to become God's thoughts.

As it turned out, I looked forward to exercising on the treadmill. It reminded me of the long walks I used to take in the fall and winter in Alabama, the beautiful, which included numerous hills, and I would program the treadmill machine to include higher inclines. By me reading Scriptures and meditating on them, sixty minutes appeared to go faster.

Then, my exercise routines included upper body twice a week and lower body twice a week. Honestly, I was very inconsistent with my upper and lower body exercises. Some weeks, I did them consistently for two or three weeks. Then, it would be months before I included them again in my regular exercise routines. Yet, I never completely forgot them. I was merely inconsistent in doing them.

Once I recommitted and rededicated my life to Jesus Christ, I began to listen and observe Angela's and Robert Jr's interactions with each other in hopes that I would understand them better. In other words, I desired to understand their world, observe how they maneuvered through the pressures they faced, and learn about those things that influenced them. I knew peer pressure from their friends and acquaintances conflicted with my views on several subjects.

There were certain children I did not want Angela and Robert Jr to associate with because of their reputations and attitudes, and it appeared that those children lacked parental influences in their actions and behaviors. Of course, I was accused of being judgmental by both of my children.

So, I would ask them which one of the three of us had lived longer and had experienced life's many years of disappointments and successes. I admitted to them that I had made some bad and some good decisions; I regretted all of my bad decisions, and I have never regretted any of my good decisions. Now, I desire to make more good decisions each day and less bad ones. I also told them that if I were raising them wrong, God would judge me and hold me accountable. In the meantime, both of them must obey me because, as their parent,

I was completely responsible for them, not their friends, acquaintances, neighbors, etc.

Because my overall behavior and attitude changed drastically for the better after I had rededicated and recommitted my life to Jesus Christ, I became more patient and more relaxed with Robert, Angela, and Robert, Jr. Their messes did not disturb me as much. I learned to live with their messes and not make a fuss about them. Whenever I had the time, I would disinfect everything we touched regularly, even when I did not have time to clean all the objects thoroughly.

My mind and attitude were being transformed. I knew I was not responsible for this transformation on my own. It was God through God's written Word. I had begun regularly praying, reading, meditating, and studying God's written Word. Finally, God was the head of my life. Through God's love, mercy, and grace, I became more confident in making decisions in every area and aspect of my life, including as a wife and parent. Each day, I was more relaxed and enjoyed each day more. I was more appreciative of the numerous small blessings God was bestowing on me each day. Merely waking up each morning was a blessing from God. Thank God!

As an active Messiah Baptist Church (MBC) member, I was engaged in numerous conversations with other church members every time I went to church. I concentrated primarily on all aspects of the Christian educational ministries, which included a variety of Bible classes. Some of those classes ranged from six weeks to two years. The new members' Bible class was Lessons on Assurance, which was the shortest. It had been many years since I had been involved in studying God's

Word. This new members' Bible class began my pursuit of developing an intimate and personal relationship with God.

Whenever I've made up my mind to do something, I've committed myself wholeheartedly. It never mattered whether it was a solo endeavor or a joint effort; I committed the same amount of time to complete each one. I was never satisfied with the results unless I knew I had done the best job I humanly possibly could.

I treated studying the Word of God like I did whenever I ventured into a new endeavor. I remember a Scripture in that first new members' Bible class that says, "We are God's workmanship, created in Christ Jesus to do good works, which God prepared in advance for us to do (Ephesians 2:10, NIV).

Since God's Word existed before the beginning of time, was true then, and remained true, I was prepared by God in advance to do good and to do good works. It was as if several lights went off in my heart and mind simultaneously. Doing good works, doing good deeds, and having good thoughts were following God's Word in obedience to God. This was not meant to be unique to believers in Jesus Christ. Each and every one of us was to do good work, and each and every one of us had already been prepared in advance to do this.

My actions should speak louder than words. My good works and deeds should speak louder than words. Others should benefit from my good works and deeds, and I should not broadcast my good works and deeds to others. Those individuals who were the recipients of my good works and deeds were supposed to spread awareness of my good works and deeds to others. Matthew 6:1 says to be careful not to do my 'acts of kindness of righteousness' before people to be seen by them (NIV, personalized).

As my journey in studying the Lessons on Assurance continued during the following six weeks, my mind was enlightened, and new spiritual knowledge was being revealed to me that I had been lacking. The more I learned about all the attributes of God, the thirstier I became to know God and to learn more. I discovered that I eagerly looked forward to talking to God (praying to God) any time of the day and night. I discovered that the five minutes I had planned and set aside for reading the Bible daily had become too brief. I began to have dreams of God…holy dreams!

And so I set aside more time just to read the Bible. I became very excited about learning about a God who loved me just as I was. And those images of me not being chosen by God dissipated from my thoughts and mind. I discovered that God had chosen the Jews to demonstrate to the world God's magnificent supernatural power through them so that all other ethnic groups of people would know that the Jews' God was the one and only true living God with all supernatural power. I discovered that no one and nothing was more powerful, loving, kind, merciful, forgiving, good, present, knowledgeable, etc., than God, the Creator…and never would be!

In the following months, I realized that my conscience had been the Holy Spirit...God's Spirit. Mama and Daddy had always said, "Let my conscience be your guide." How was I to know that my conscience was the Holy Spirit?

Although I had neglected to honor God on a daily basis for many years, I finally figured out that whenever I had had difficult decisions to make and followed what my conscience said, I had done the right things, and when I did not follow my conscious, I had done the wrong things. I wished that when Mama and Daddy had been raising and nurturing me, they had used the words Holy Spirit rather than my conscious. Knowing that God had been with me every day and every hour all my life instilled confidence in me that I never had before.

It was no wonder that I had felt that there had been a tremendous lack in my life. Henceforth, I can do all things through Christ, who strengthens me (Philippians 4:13, WEB). Without me knowing this and up to that period of time, I had felt powerless and that the white folks had more power than black and brown folks. God desires to bless all of God's people abundantly, because God is love and always will be love. Therefore, I began to thank God for life and freedom in Jesus Christ from them on, and I've never looked back. Although I wished I had discovered and been aware of the love of God much earlier, I had grown tired of songs that made me feel like poor little me, and I did not desire any part of a poor God, as I had said previously. It appeared to me that some believers preferred a poor God because of their behaviors, actions, and the prayers I heard them pray. I am by no means being judgmental of others. Yet, actions speak louder than words.

As the one and only true living God, God could have chosen another way to come from heaven, yet God in the form of the incarnate Jesus was borne to an unwed fourteen-year-old teenager and Joseph, a carpenter, as his parents and placed in an animal trough soon after his birth rather than a baby's crib. The incarnated Jesus could have come from a wealthy family. If so, multitudes of people would have been excluded. God loves all people, and everybody has equal access to God. For God does not show favoritism and for there is no respect of persons with God (Romans 2:11, NIV, and KJ V).

As I continued to study God's Word, the yokes that had been placed around my mind and neck were slowly and consistently being loosened and broken. Once those yokes had been broken completely, I was indeed free! I may have looked the same on the outside; I may have walked the same on the outside, but I had been transformed on the inside by the renewing of my mind, which resulted in me being able to test and approve what God's will for my life-God's good, pleasing and perfect will (Romans 12:2b-c, NIV, personalized).

5
Rising to the Occasions

I urge you, brothers and sisters, to watch out for those who cause divisions and put obstacles in your way that are contrary to the teaching you have learned. Keep away from them (Romans 16:17, NIV).

When Angela graduated from high school, she was seventeen, and I was thirty-six. Today, many married couples are having their first child in their mid-thirties. There I was at age thirty-six with a high school graduate who would be entering college in the fall. Where had the time gone? I was so busy with life each day that I turned thirty-six without worrying and thinking about approaching forty in four years. When I turned thirty, I attended Tufts University School of Dental Medicine (TUSDM), and I had no time to dwell on leaving my twenties and entering my thirties. I knew I had had a birthday each year. Yet, my life was moving along rapidly, and I felt I would not have time to do everything I needed and desired.

Because I had not been educated in the Boston Schools, I had no idea who I should consult about college at age seventeen, and the process of applying for college scholarships and federal grants was completely foreign to me. It took me six years, from 1965 until 1971, to connect with individuals willing to guide me through applying to colleges. Therefore, I took an indirect route instead of a direct one. I realized that I needed to take refresher courses before applying to college. I settled for Odwin Health Careers on Dimock Street, Roxbury, Massachusetts, in order to accomplish this necessary endeavor.

All of the refresher courses were free, and the instructors spent tireless hours teaching and mentoring me for several months so that I would be successful once I was attending college. I had tremendous confidence that I would master every stumbling block I encountered in each college course, and this was mainly attributed to the exemplary teaching, mentoring, and tutoring of my former teachers at Odwin Health Careers. Every one of them was gifted to teach. It was as if each one had an invested interest in my success, and they did. My teachers at Odwin Health Careers celebrated each of my accomplishments as parents celebrated their children's successes. I am so very grateful that Angela did not have to experience the difficulties of preparing for college as I did.

At age seven, Robert and I took Robert Jr to camp, which lasted for six weeks. We visited him biweekly on Sundays. On our first biweekly visit, I did not recognize our son. Robert had to point him out to me. Robert Jr was so ashy and dry, with uncombed hair and dry lips. Once I knew that strange-looking boy was actually my son, I called out to him loudly. I wanted to take him to his cabin, lotion him down, comb his hair, and put Vaseline on his lips. Robert said, “Leave the boy alone. He’s having the time of his life.” I did as Robert requested, and the three of us went and had lunch together and talked. Robert

Jr even taught me a short rhyme that he had learned as all of the camp counselors and campers sat around the camp fires.

The rhyme went like this: Now, there was grandma swinging from the outhouse door, wearing a nightie, and grandpa saying, "More and more." Now, I thought it was just a silly and funny rhyme, and I laughed at that silly and funny rhyme until my eyes teared up. In my mind, I was imagining an old lady swinging on an outhouse door and how funny she must have looked. It was obvious to Robert that grandpa had other things on his mind, so he only smiled.

Later, Robert explained to me precisely what that rhyme meant, and I was stunned. I thought to myself that I was still very naïve about many things. I was perplexed as to why would a bunch of camp counselors teach young boys such a sexual rhyme. I never discussed the rhyme with Robert Jr. I left the matter in Robert's hands. Besides, I was unsure if Robert Jr was just naïve like I was in the eighth grade when my friend Irma had taught me a sexual rhyme without knowing it was sexual or was it something boys learned early just because of their gender. Either way, father, and son were the same gender, and I felt Robert would understand Robert Jr's mindset at his current age much better than I could.

In preparing for college, Angela took her SATs in the spring of her junior year and scored so well on them that she did not need to retake them again. Angela demonstrated brilliancy in school as long as she applied herself. She had done all of the research on the different colleges and universities during her junior year of high school. So, she was very well prepared to apply for college in a timely fashion in her senior year. Angela chose to attend an all-women's college in western

Massachusetts, one of the three colleges close to each other. I was very pleased with Angela's choice, because it would only take me an hour and forty-five minutes to arrive at her college.

During the summer after Angela graduated from high school, she and I were very busy shopping for clothes, shoes, boots, coats, bed linens, towels, etc. We enjoyed going out on our shopping sprees. By the time, it was time to take Angela to college, we couldn't fit everything in the car, and we decided that I would make a second trip and bring the remaining items out to her within a couple of weeks. Angela was very excited about living in the dorm and being away from home.

I believe I was just as excited as Angela about attending college. In fact, I was very relieved that Angela was away at college and no longer living at home full-time. I had been extremely stressed about Angela's attitude toward me, and I felt like I was walking on eggshells when Robert was not at home. It seemed that everything I said or did caused Angela to be upset. I was hoping that Angela would miss me and begin to realize that she did not hate me. At least, now we had breathing space between us, which was an hour and forty-five minutes in distance by car.

With Angela away in college, I felt such a great sense of relief I had not experienced in years. I could breathe a little better, and I was much more relaxed. I reminisced about Angela and my experiences together over the last seventeen years as mother and daughter, and I acknowledged to myself that every minute had been worth it. And being thirty-six had become just another number as far as I was concerned. Therefore, I would become more engaged with parenting Robert Jr. Therefore, I continued preparing his breakfast for him each morning as usual, and I decided to remain with Robert Jr in the kitchen until he finished his breakfast every morning.

As I remained in the kitchen while Robert Jr ate his breakfast each morning, I was unaware that Robert Jr was storing up fond memories of his childhood. Many years later, he told me that eating his breakfast, which consisted of hot oatmeal with milk, buttered toast, and orange juice, as I sat at the table opposite him or stood leaning against a kitchen counter was one of his fondest childhood memories. And to think that my simple act of being completely dressed to leave the house each morning before preparing Robert Jr's breakfast had resulted in one of his treasured childhood memories was amazing. As soon as Robert Jr had left the house and walked down to his school bus stop with some of his friends, I hurriedly left the house each morning.

During Angela's first year in college, one of my sisters needed my help with her five children. I met with the judge and agreed to be responsible for my five nieces and nephews as long as they needed me. I did not have time to discuss this matter with Robert in advance. I just showed up in court before the judge to prevent my five nieces and nephews from becoming wards of the court.

After my two nieces and one nephew were safely home with me, I called Robert and told him what had occurred. Robert agreed that I had made the right decision. Angela's bedroom was converted into a room for my two nieces and one nephew. They were ages twelve, nine, and two. The twin boys were ages six and a half months and were still in the hospital recovering from smoke inhalation.

To be honest, I felt overwhelmed with the responsibilities of taking care of five children, and my son made six. It was deja vu for me again. You see, after my two older sisters left home, I was given the responsibilities they had when I was merely nine years old.

Although I already had a busy and full life, I had to rise to the occasion of raising and nurturing my nieces and nephews since there was no one else to do it. I thanked God that I had an intimate and personal relationship with God, because I knew I would fail miserably without it. It was God who gave me the strength each day to care for my nieces and nephews. And thankfully, I had rededicated and recommitted my life to Jesus Christ earlier. Otherwise, I honestly believe I would not have consented to appear before the judge to accept the guardianship of my five nieces and nephews because I never desired a house full of children in my home 24/7.

As I went about shopping for clothes, shoes, sleeping bags, linen, pillows, two baby cribs, formulas, diapers, bottles, pacifiers, infant car seats, etc., I turned my attention to making arrangements to pick-up my twin nephews from the hospital.

Considering all of the circumstances, my nieces and nephews adjusted well in our home. I must admit it was a lot of work and took up much of my time. I was thankful that it took Robert only two weeks to recover from the shock of having six children in the house.

By the way, Robert had slept in the family room for two weeks, located two flights down from our bedroom. After two weeks, he fully participated in parenting all six children. Robert Jr was the only one who enjoyed having five additional children in our home from the beginning. He and my two nieces were very close in age...one was a year older and a year younger than Robert Jr. He had instant playmates 24/7, and he was thrilled.

Enrolling my two nieces in school was somewhat of a challenge. I did not have any school information requested by the Easton School administration in order to make their school transfers proceed smoothly. So, I explained to the school administration that I had become their guardian because of an urgent family emergency. And after listening to my explanations, both nieces were permitted to attend classes that same day.

As I was responsible for dressing three nephews every morning and dropping them off at the childcare provider, I worked full days in my dental office, treating patients. The childcare provider was very kind, patient, and understanding. She was amazed that I had undertaken such a tremendous responsibility of taking care of five children, because I already had a full and busy work schedule treating dental patients, and two nights each week, I worked until 9:00pm in my dental practice.

At the end of the school year, my two nieces and one nephew were returned to their mother, and Robert and I continued parenting my twin nephews. They were with us all the time...Sunday School, worship services, vacations, etc. Often, I waited until Robert was home to go grocery shopping. Although Robert Jr was only twelve years old, I left him home with my twin nephews on a few occasions as I rushed to the supermarket. I did what I had to do to manage those demanding responsibilities without going out of my mind.

When my twin nephews were eighteen months old, they were returned to their mother. I wanted to hire a lawyer to implement a legal fight to keep my sister from regaining custody of her twin boys. After much prayer, I returned them to their mother. I was saddened for several months afterward. Robert and Robert Jr were saddened, too. Eventually, our sadness ceased, and we frequently reminisced about my nephews with fond memories and joy in our hearts and minds. Robert and I admitted that all the hard work required of us was worth every minute, and we had no regrets.

Since Angela was away at college, her routine was not affected much. She was only home for some weekends and school breaks. Otherwise, Angela continued to enjoy college life.

As Robert Jr was approaching adolescent, Robert decided to keep him busy by purchasing him three-wheelers and four-wheelers, known officially as all-terrain vehicles, and they would go to the sand pit to ride them. Robert knew just what and how to keep our son from being bored. Robert Jr was involved in year-round sports and had been active in Easton Pop Warner since age seven. Robert Jr often asked me to ride with him to the sand pit. I kindly refused every time he asked me, because I witnessed Robert and Robert Jr's appearances every time they returned from their trips to the sand pit. They had sand on their faces, in their hair, on their bodies, and in their clothes and sneakers. I wanted no part of being dirty like they were.

Every time they returned to the house, they made a huge mess leading from the patio into the living room, and both were oblivious to the mess they made each time. While attempting to figure out how to improve my parenting skills with Robert Jr., I felt that Robert instinctively knew what to do with and for him. Although I had taken Robert Jr on his first fishing trip at the age of four, Robert took him fishing frequently, and I avoided all future fishing trips with Robert Jr. Although, I do remember going fishing with Robert once. That fishing venture was very boring and smelly, and Robert informed me that I was frightening away the fish because I was constantly talking. I asked Robert to exclude me from all of his future fishing trips, and he has. I encouraged Robert to invite his friends who enjoyed fishing…male and female. He followed my advice.

When Robert Jr began misbehaving in ways I had never experienced, I attributed that to him being a boy. Since I was a girl, Robert Jr's behavior was totally foreign to me. Robert Jr's behavior was beyond my understanding. I took him to the altar on many Sundays for prayer during alter calls. I even took him to Pastor Walker on many Sundays for prayer when altar calls were not scheduled.

During one of my conversations with Robert Jr, he told me I did not know anything about football, and he was correct. The point was that I was not discussing football with him at that time, and that was his way of informing me without being disrespectful that he was not accepting my advice. My response to him was, "You are so right. I know nothing about football, but I know someone who does."

When Robert arrived home later, I told him the entire scenario, and henceforth, Robert made sure he was present for Robert, Jr. Robert kept watchful eyes on Robert, Jr whether he liked it or not. Practically everyone in Easton who knew Robert could recognize Robert Jr as Robert's son. Since Robert was an

Easton business owner, sponsored Pop Warner athletic teams each year, was a member of Easton Chambers of Commerce, belonged to the Easton Lions Club, and attended every one of Robert Jr's games, he was well-known throughout Easton.

Frequently, Robert Jr was escorted back to Robert's business during his adolescent years by the Easton police. Robert often observed Robert Jr in his all-terrain vehicles (ATVs) being followed by a police officer in a police cruiser. He shared with me that he would smile to himself every time that happened, thanked the police officer, and calmly reminded Robert Jr to ride his ATV on acceptable trails and not on the streets.

Eventually, all of Robert Jr's infarctions of being caught riding his ATV on the street stopped. As it turned out, he had discovered old railroad tracks that lead from Easton to New Bedford, Massachusetts, and off he went on numerous unsupervised and without parental consent adventures to New Bedford on his ATV. Robert Jr said he would schedule those trips to New Bedford during the day while his daddy was working. He made sure that he returned home before his daddy arrived home in the evenings. Robert Jr told me he was never concerned with me finding out because my job and school commitments were in Boston. Of course, Robert and I were unaware of Robert Jr's trips to New Bedford until he was an adult and living independently.

When Robert and I were raising Angela and Robert Jr, there were no cell phones or social media venues. They had land phones and TVs in their bedrooms.

As a trusting mother, the majority of the time, they abided by the rules of no phone calls and no TV privileges until their school work was completed. I believe Angela and Robert Jr frequently continued talking on the phone and watching TV well beyond their bedtime. Yet, as long as they were up, dressed, on time the next day, turned in their school assignments on time, participated in class discussions, and did well on their quizzes and examinations, I did not feel the need to check on them. I called it trust. And I still call it trust.

Years later, both of them shared some of the things they did once I was sound asleep. Angela and Robert Jr said they frequently sneaked out of the house through the patio doors in the middle of the night. Other times, they would drive my car to Burger King for fast food without my permission. I have no regrets about trusting them. I believed they were extra careful not to get into trouble, so I would not stop trusting them. I am quite sure there are numerous infractions Angela and Robert, Jr committed as teenagers that they considered good and clean fun that I would never know about…it's called growing up.

The pervasive and prevalent perils children face growing up in today's toxic environments are concerning. There was a time when people in the community kept their watchful eyes on all children. The adults honored and readily followed an unwritten obligation to keep all children safe from the evil ones and from themselves. Back in the day, it was called the village…it takes a village to raise each child. Numerous children growing up these days don't understand the concept that it takes a village to raise each child, and many adults have relinquished their responsibilities of investing their time and efforts in watching over the welfare of their children and the children of others.

As time passed, Robert Jr. constantly shared with me the many negative trends he and his wife have combatted regarding the toxic policies and programs being promoted through those persons in key positions in our political, educational, economic, and financial positions. Due to the prevalent use of high-tech devices and different alternate news sources that are readily available and accessible to their children, they have struggled to counteract those negative influences on their children. Children do not have good vetting skills, and they need responsible parents and adults regularly to nurture and guide them in their decisions.

My sympathy goes out to parents raising their children in these toxic environments throughout the world. My two children were latch-key children, and it never entered my mind that something harmful would happen to them just by being involved in good and clean fun with their friends. There have always been a variety of crimes in the world dating back to Biblical times. Now, parents are struggling with the influence of social media on their children. Back in the day, I knew that movies and TV programs were purely for my entertainment.

By the age of ten, countless children already have their own cell phones, and many have access to Twitter, Instagram, Meta, etc., by the age of thirteen. Children trust what they read and hear on social media more than what their parents and guardians teach them. Even two of my adult grandchildren have been led astray, along with millions of other children. I don't have any answers to my adult children's dilemma regarding their children believing what Qanon theorists promote. I only have difficult questions!

Unfortunately, many parents are the culprits in their own children's demise, because some parents are not disconnecting from their high-tech devices either and are being influenced by all types of alternate news sources.

What happened to face-to-face conversations between people? Long before the COVID-19 pandemic occurred, many generations of people had lost the skills required for effective face-to-face communication. This loss of effective communication skills became evident and prevalent when greater use of emails came into existence. As long as there is an ongoing COVID-19 pandemic, in-person conversations in close proximity should be avoided or at least limited whenever possible. Hopefully, face-to-face conversations between people will significantly increase once COVID-19 becomes endemic and annual COVID-19 shots are recommended.

Since I would rather not engage in casual conversations over the phone, I eagerly look forward to greeting and talking with people face-to-face without any apprehension about breakthrough COVID-19 cases. In the future, all of us will have to learn to co-exist with COVID-19 and its variants just as we've learned to co-exist with the common cold and flu.

As I remain a highly committed germophobe, I have consistently practiced the recommended COVID-19 mitigations for two years and counting. Until I am convinced there is no need to wear face masks, I will continue to do so…to each their own.

Of course, I am tired of the restrictions, just like millions of other folks. But, when I think of the options, which are the risk of catching COVID-19, being hospitalized due to COVID-19, living as a long hauler after COVID-19, dying from

COVID-19, etc., I have continued following the recommended mitigations of reputable public health experts by wearing double face masks, wearing disposable gloves in the supermarkets, and social distancing. I would much rather be overly cautious than not being cautious enough. Proverbs 3:3-6 says to trust in the Lord with all my heart and not lean on my understanding. In all my ways, acknowledge God, and God will make my path straight (NIV, personalized).

6
My Regrets and Joys

Then I acknowledged my sin to you and did not cover up my iniquity.

I said, "I will confess my transgressions to the LORD." And you forgave the guilt of my sin (Psalm 32:5, NIV).

Rejoice in the Lord always. I will say it again: Rejoice! (Philippians 4:3, NIV).

One of my regrets is the fact that I neglected to have my two children dedicated before an altar in a church officiated by an ordained minister in the presence of my family, friends, and church members. I realize now that I would have had loads of people who would have readily assisted me in my parenting skills and provided spiritual and hands-on support. I struggled through many years with the tremendous responsibilities of parenting on my own, with much regret.

When Robert and I were unhappily married, I often wondered if Angela was affected negatively during her preadolescent and early teenage years. Although we kept our arguments to a minimum in her presence, Angela sensed something was wrong between her daddy and me. I wanted Angela to have a happy childhood, and I became concerned she had been affected over the years. Although I tried my best to keep my unhappiness a secret from Angela and Robert, Jr, I believe I failed miserably to my regret. I still say that Mama and Daddy handled their tough times much better than I did. God bless them!

For seven years, Angela was the only child and the apple of my eye. Everything I brought into the home for a child was for Angela for seven years. She did not have to share her clothes, toys, and books. They belonged to only Angela. When other children came to play with Angela, she readily shared her toys, and I did not observe any selfish behavior at all. Angela figured it all out that her toys would remain with her long after her friends had gone home.

As long as Robert Jr was a baby and could not crawl, Angela doted on her brother. She even wanted to help dress him and play games with him. Angela would entertain her baby brother for long periods of time as they laughed together, and she was never tired of holding him in her lap. Angela would frequently have story time just for her baby brother. It was as if Robert and I had her baby brother just for her. Angela was very proud to have a baby brother and never mentioned that she regretted having a brother since she had initially expressed her desire for a sister.

For several months after Robert Jr was born, Robert and I had been attempting to figure out the best time to explain to Angela about her birth. I was very worried that if we did not inform Angela soon, she would discover the truth intentionally or unintentionally by someone else intentionally. I did not want

Angela to be hurt in any way. When Robert and I finally had this conversation with Angela, she asked many questions, and we took the time to answer them truthfully.

This was one of the most difficult conversations of my life. I was concerned that Angela would grow up feeling bad about herself and refuse to share her true feelings with her daddy or me. I was very protective of Angela then; I remain overly protective of Angela and always will. In my mind, I have rejected all possibilities that the rapist could have given Angela any defective genetic DNA. She has not had any involvement with him, does not know him, and has never seen him. I have claimed that Angela inherited all the good genes God purposely planned in her, and I believe this wholeheartedly. Thank God!

Unfortunately, there have been millions of children born as a result of their mothers being raped, and these heinous crimes committed against their mothers were never said to the children born as a result of those rapes. After rededicating and recommitting my life to Jesus Christ, I have constantly prayed to God for Angela's well-being, for her to embrace everything concerning her birth, and just to trust and believe that God has never made any mistakes in the method God chose for her to be borne, even before the beginning of time. Praise God!

Once Angela had been told the truth about her birth, I discovered there had been much resentment between Robert Jr and her, and this resentment was based on the fact that Robert was not her biological daddy. And because of the way Angela felt, I was even more protective of her. I tried my best to compensate for all of the insecurities that she would be experiencing, and most of the time, I did not know what was the best approach to take. I hugged Angela frequently and praised her daily. I made efforts not to burden Angela with babysitting Robert Jr unless I had no other alternative. I never asked Angela to babysit Robert Jr when I was home, although I could have used her help.

Except for the times I took Angela to church as a toddler, to my friend Diane's church, and when I was a visitor at different Methodist and Baptist churches, Angela's early childhood was primarily void of being taught about God's love for her. I had never included any children's Biblical books to read to her. I believe Angela's older child provider, my sister, Carrie, and sister-in-law, Elnora, taught Angela the children's prayer and the Lord's prayer during the first four years of her life. Regrettably, I know I had not. Since Angela attended parochial school in the first and second grades, maybe the nuns taught her about baby Jesus and the love of God for her.

I still regret that during the time when Angela was growing and developing in my womb, I did not know that God loved me. I still believe that because of my insecurities, doubts, fears, anger at God, and anger and hate toward the rapist that some of those feelings were transmitted to Angela. I hope and pray Angela has found total acceptance and peace with her birth. If not, I still depend on and trust God to always take good care of my innocent daughter with God's love, mercy, and grace each day.

In addition, I regret that I missed out on the joy of knowing God from the time I was raped until the time I rededicated and recommitted my life to Jesus Christ. At the age of eighteen, I was innocent of people's evil ways, except for the haters. I had not and never have been involved with the criminal justice system. Although the hippies were smoking marijuana, Cassie, our friends, and I were not interested in doing any of those things that were against what our parents had taught us.

Besides, we did not associate with any hippies. I don't recall ever seeing any face to face, although the movies we attended had plenty of hippies smoking marijuana, multiple sexual partners, and living in communes. And that type of lifestyle did not interest us. I related the hippies' lifestyles with the children of the rich and wealthy people. Children of wealthy parents could afford to be sent them abroad to expensive spas and treatment programs to overcome their addictions.

Cassie and I would end up with criminal records that would impede our educational aspirations, if we were caught in the wrong places at the wrong time, even if we were not involved in any unlawful activities. Whenever we were not working and attending classes at night, Cassie and I spent our leisure time studying and having good, clean fun on weekends. We did not even know anyone smoking marijuana, and the thought of associating with individuals using any drugs or injecting heroin was completely foreign to us.

I frequented the movies purely for entertainment purposes and never to incorporate the actions of the movie stars into my personal life. To me, the movies were fantasies and were meant to be enjoyed and not duplicated in my life.

I have come to terms with the fact that I endured much shame, embarrassment, and mistreatment in my lifetime, and those shameful events, embarrassments, and mistreatments do not define me and never have.

Because I was crippled emotionally as a result of the rape, I did not behave as well as a mother Angela deserved, although

I was doing the best I knew how on my own understanding. Daily morning and evening prayers were absent in my life, because I had chosen to eliminate them. At that time, I did not realize that I was missing out on the relationship I needed with God, and I did not realize that I was inflicting potential harm to my baby's relationship with God and her desire to seek God.

As a matter of fact, I don't remember ever reading the Bible and praying in Angela's presence until she was a teenager, although I did attend church worship services with her. But, during that period, I did not attend any Sunday School or Bible study classes. Angela did observe me reading numerous books, though. They were never Christian-based.

Because Angela attended a parochial school in the first and second grades, learning the Bible was an integral part of her education, just as all of the other core courses were, and there was a priest who prayed for all of the students at the beginning of each school day.

Every accomplishment Angela achieved was treated as a grand achievement on my part, and I would ask Angela what type of reward she wanted. Usually, her responses were very reasonable. Angela enjoyed school just as much as I had from an early age. She never wanted to miss any school days. Her many friends attended the same school; I could relate to that because my close friends and I also attended the same school.

On the other hand, I was never very concerned about Robert, Jr. in the same way as I was concerned about Angela. Robert Jr never had blank spaces on his birth certificate, and he never had to live a day in his life without two adoring and devoted parents. The truth about his birth would never hurt him.

It was as if Robert Jr had been born with high self-esteem and self-confidence.

The Easton Journal newspaper had begun writing about Robert, Jr, the second year he played football on the Easton Pop Warner team. Robert Jr.'s football coaches said there were some things they could not teach Robert Jr…he just had natural abilities that no one could teach. Robert and I had to make sure that Robert Jr did not develop a mega ego and think too highly of himself. In other words, we wanted him to demonstrate humility, not brag and boast about his accomplishments. We were very proud of Robert Jr and told him so.

So, one could imagine that an eight-year-old boy could very quickly develop a swelled head and think too highly of himself. Robert and I knew Robert Jr was talented, and we encouraged him to be the best he could be at whatever endeavor he chose to do. Robert Jr was very good at swimming and track. He was an average player in basketball and baseball.

During the Pop Warner football season, when Robert Jr was in seventh grade, I fired him from the football team. I instructed Robert Jr to tell his coach, Mr. Powers, that I was his head coach, and I only allowed him to coach my son, because I did not know enough about football. I discovered that Robert Jr was not performing at his best in school, and as his punishment, he had to forgo football for the entire season. In addition, Robert Jr had to spend three hours each weekday at the library reading for the entire summer.

Some people may think I was too hard on Robert, Jr. Yet, I was not, and I still don't regret the punishment I doled out to him. I tell you that I believe Robert Jr learned a valuable lesson from his punishment…he had to earn the privilege of playing football. Henceforth, he kept his grades up to a level the next year that pleased me, and he played football and enjoyed playing again. The Easton Journal mentioned something about Robert, Jr in each of their edition. And he became a local celebrity. Thankfully, Pastor Walker had invited recruiters from Thayer Academy to give a presentation about the school. So, Robert and I decided to enroll Robert Jr in a private school. He took the independent entrance examination and was accepted to Thayer Academy for his four years of high school.

Robert Jr had a different idea about where he would be attending school. He had decided that he would not do his best academically, so we would withdraw him from Thayer Academy after seeing his first term report card. The joke was on him. Robert and I firmly told him that we don't accept C grades. We knew he was capable of getting higher than Cs, if he had tried his best. And besides, we were already paying our taxes that helped fund the Easton Public Schools, and we were paying Thayer Academy.

Since Robert and I didn't accept C grades from Easton Public School, we definitely wouldn't accept C grades from a private school. After that talk we had with Robert Jr, he got his act together and began earning mainly A grades with one or two B grades for the remainder of his freshman year of high school.

Not only did Robert Jr take his education seriously, but he chose to study and complete all of his school assignments in the dining room; he removed his TV and Nintendo from his bedroom and decided that his bedroom would only be for sleeping. All of his teachers noticed the changes Robert Jr was exhibiting. By the time Robert Jr graduated from Thayer

Academy, he had broken several past football records and established new ones and graduated cum laude. He was also honored by winning the headmasters' award for exemplifying the ideal experience of a Thayer Academy student.

When Angela and her husband presented me with my first grandson, John, I was only forty-one years of age. I thought I was too young to be a grandmother, because I was still working full-time and trying to figure out which divinity program I should apply to since God had called me to preach the year before.

Isaiah 55:8-9 says for God's thoughts are not my thoughts, neither are God's ways my ways. As the heavens are higher than the earth, so are God's ways higher than my ways and God's thoughts than my thoughts (NIV, personalized). God knew that I needed a special person full of God's wisdom, knowledge, and understanding all along. I know for a fact that it would take a person who was wiser than my natural wisdom to get my attention.

At that juncture in my life, I had had my fill of people who had merely talked the talk, but their lives did not reveal that they were living their talk. To me, they meant to do what they did, and not what they said. It was as if they acted and lived one way on Sundays, but they lived different ways the remaining six days each week. I felt that I could have done better without people like that in my personal life. I wanted people in my personal life to accept me just as I was and help me to become a better person in every area of my life. I desired people to admit that they were not perfect and never would become perfect, but they would try to do better and better.

As I was walking one morning in 1985, I decided to venture out and walk down streets I had never walked before. Lo and behold, I also met Deacon Lillian walking alone. We introduced ourselves to each other and continued walking together. Deacon Lillian and I decided to walk again in the mornings, because we had enjoyed talking together. We continued walking together for several months. It was a time in my life when I needed a very wise spiritual woman in my life.

Although Deacon Lillian was not a fast walker, I got in the habit of meeting up with her on the two mornings my work days began at 11:00 am. It was not long before we were sharing our authentic selves with each other. Since she was older, wiser, and very spiritual, I confided in her about my concerns about my two children. She was never judgmental and guided me in the right direction on many issues. Deacon Lillian added my name to her prayer list and told me about the Wednesday prayer meetings and Thursday night healing and blessing services. After getting to know each other, I was invited to attend her church.

As time passed, I informed Deacon Lillian that I had attended Messiah Baptist Church (MBC) years earlier when Rev. Neville was the pastor, and she said, "MBC has a new pastor from Texas, and he sure can preach." Sometimes, when I had attended MBC, I took Angela and Robert Jr with me. Deacon Lillian was the first person I had become comfortable with enough to share and ask questions I desired answers to in many years. It felt good to have a confidant and not be concerned about hearing about my confidential information being violated. Some of the issues we discussed would violate the confidential information she shared with me, even now. Therefore, I refuse to. Deacon Lillian helped in more ways than one, and I am very grateful to have had her in my life in times of need.

Well, on a wintery day in January, I met someone who would be instrumental in changing my life forever. I had taken Daddy to Sunday School and worship service at that time, because I had promised him. As it turned out, that day began a life-changing experience that has been ongoing for many decades.

That special and unique person was The Rev. Michael Wayne Walker. I have never been my old self after meeting him on that cold wintery day in January. One week later to that day, I became a new creation in Jesus Christ. It was not that I had never had a relationship with Jesus Christ before, since I had grown up attending church. I had turned my back on God and God's Word for more years than I would like to admit.

Throughout those years, I had only called upon the Lord when I needed God's help for a task for which I felt that my own strength was insufficient. I needed God's supernatural power. In dental school, God had answered many of my prayers for the correct selections of those multiple-choice questions and for those tough oral questions my oral surgery professor asked me in the oral surgery operating room at Tufts University School of Dental Medicine (TUSD). I surprised myself when I answered his questions correctly. Henceforth, my oral surgery professor assumed I knew all the answers and never asked me questions again.

Because of my horrible past experience when I was eighteen years old, I protected my personal space and was hesitant to become friendly with any men. And I had made sure that I was never alone with them. From that first meeting,

Pastor Walker was different, and he made eye-to-eye contact when he asked me the question, which was, what about the doctor? Although I was lost for words on that day, Pastor Walker captured my attention, which I have never forgotten, and I remain eternally grateful to him for being so direct.

As it turned out, God used Pastor Walker to accept me just as I was and helped me realize God's purpose for me. By the time I was eighteen, I had at least ten different pastors because I had a Methodist background. In the Methodist church, the bishops decided on the length of time a pastor remained in that honored position as pastor.

As a Baptist church member, I had opportunities to meet with a pastor who lived the way he talked seven days a week. And I took advantage of those opportunities and revealed everything to Pastor Walker. For the first time in many years, I had found a person similar to Daddy, although much younger than Daddy in years.

I often felt that God had spoken to Pastor Walker about what was on my mind before we met. He revealed to me that God had told him on Thursday that he would be meeting me, a doctor, on Sunday when I showed up at Messiah Baptist Church (MBC). And he had just taken God at God's Word. I was dumbfounded and kept quiet with a frozen wide smile on my face. I was relieved when Daddy asked me if we would be attending the fellowship gathering. I apologized to Daddy, excused myself, and escorted Daddy to the fellowship hall for refreshments. Daddy needed to have a small snack as soon as possible after the worship service because he had diabetes.

Through Daddy, God's love had drawn me back into God's loving arms, and Pastor Walker was God's vessel to teach me what I needed to know patiently. My thirst to know God better was like I had taken energy pills. Yet, I had not taken any medication of any kind. I was high on God…a supernatural high and the only high that was good for me in every way.

My outlook had changed, and I was eager to learn more and more about God through God's Word, and I recognized the anointing God had given Pastor Walker. God had chosen the best pastor God had just for me, and I needed a servant of God who was totally committed to honoring God in every aspect of his life.

As it turned out, when Daddy had come to live with Robert and me, Messiah Baptist Church (MBC) was the church I took him to. And it was because Deacon Lillian had frequently talked to me about her pastor's preaching. Deacon Lillian made sure Daddy was present at every healing and blessing service on Thursdays since Thursdays were one of the evenings I worked late in my dental practice.

Once I became a Messiah Baptist Church (MBC) member, God provided me with another older, wiser, and spiritual woman, Deacon Ramona. Now, I had two special people who cared about me, and she added me to her prayer list. I quickly became very comfortable with Deacon Ramona, because she was my Bible class teacher. In no time, I asked her to pray for my husband and me. My entire family was lifted up regularly in prayer services on Wednesdays. I felt good about having others praying for my family and me. I felt empowered and excited about my life and life in general.

During one of my reflection moments, the poem Footprints in the Sand came to mind. Although the authorship of Footprints in the Sand has been disputed, I continue to find comfort in it every time I read it. This poem reminds me of my life from the age of eighteen until I was in my thirties. I had felt that God did not love me nor care about me as the Bible said. And I had endured many low and sad times for several years without experiencing the presence of God. At one point in the poem, the man questioned God about where God was when he needed God. And God replied, "My son, my precious child, I love you, and I would never leave you. During your times of trial and suffering, when you only saw one set of footprints, it was I who carried you."

Oftentimes, I cried as I was reading the poem Footprints in the Sand because I could relate to the content of the man's dream. But it was my reality rather than a dream until Angela was a teenager before I reestablished an intimate and personal relationship with God.

As it turned out, I had been placed under the tutelage of the best pastor I had ever had at the right time in my life, and I was still in my thirties. I believed the best part of my life was yet to come, and I desired a full and complete life in Christ Jesus. Thank God! I remain grateful to God every day and in every way. Thank God for Pastor Walker, and thank you, Pastor Michael Wayne Walker, for being truthful in your responses. And I needed authenticity from you even when I asked you those tough questions.

Those few times when Pastor Walker truthfully said he did not know the answers, my pastor remained authentic and told God all about me. I felt his prayers and thanked Pastor Walker for consistently including me in his prayers. I know I unloaded much onto Pastor Walker...he always had a willing mind to listen to me and an able God to guide him. Proverbs 13:20 says we who walk with the wise grow wise, but a companion of fools suffer harm (N.I.V., paraphrased).

Comparing our parents' financial and educational situations with Robert's and me, God had provided us the knowledge and opportunities to guide, encourage, and challenge our two children to perform their best and become their best in the endeavors they undertook.

My heart was full when Angela graduated from college and then from two law schools, fulfilling her aspiration of becoming an attorney since the age of eight. My heart was also full when Robert Jr graduated from college, graduated from graduate school with a Master of Education degree, and began teaching mathematics and science to eighth grade school children. Robert Jr. had a challenging time in math as a youngster; he disliked reading with a passion, and now he has chosen to teach math. Robert Jr informed me years ago that he had decided not to let the challenges of mastering math get the best of him. And he did just that.

With God, all things are possible. Angela and Robert Jr graduated from high school and entered college. They did not have to be concerned about money for college, room, and board, spending cash, etc. Robert and I had taught them that they would attend college directly after graduating from high school at a very early age. Angela and Robert Jr had no time to get lost, because they focused on what they would like to be doing once they were adults and living independently from us. Robert and I conditioned Angela and Robert Jr to appreciate higher learning and strive to acquire as much education as possible.

Both of my adult children are highly educated and in professions of their choosing, and they are producers rather than merely consumers in the world. I desired that my children would never have to experience the hardships I had endured in my pursuit of becoming a doctor, and they did not. Philippians 4:19 says that this same God who takes care of me will supply all of Angela's and Robert Jr's needs from God's glorious riches, which have been given to us in Christ Jesus (N.L.T., personalized).

The first glance of, my first grandchild, John, was love at first sight, and I felt as if it was all my idea for Angela and my son-in-law to become parents. Being a grandmother was even better than being a parent. I could just enjoy my grandson. I would give him everything he wanted and what I thought he wanted and needed.

Then, I would take him home to his parents whenever I was exhausted. I felt that God's plan for making me a grandmother was to bring more joy into my life, and God's plan had been successfully accomplished. I even went as far as to request the church secretary to include in the church's bulletin that my grandson had no problem nursing his mother's breasts. My grandson had been born a professional in breastfeeding. I found myself telling everyone who was willing to listen about my grandson.

As he got older, I discovered that John was very intelligent and pronounced, using words in sentences beyond his years. My daughter was the same way as her son. I remember that one day, Angela had been listening to her Aunt Cassie's conversation with a friend, and afterward, she told Cassie's friend that his explanation was impossible. Cassie could not help but laugh out loud and tell her friend that he should be ashamed of himself because he could not convince a two-year-old to believe him.

In addition, John had a childcare provider, MaryAnn, who he lovingly called NaNa, who taught him the children's prayer and the Lord's prayers at a very young age, and she took him to weekly Wednesday prayer service. John grew up participating in the prayer service at a very young age. He was very familiar with baby Jesus, because his NaNa taught him. John was very fortunate to have two grandmothers...one maternal grandmother and a God-given one by the name of MaryAnn.

In reflection, I acted as if I were the only one who had become a grandmother. I just could not keep my joy to myself. My joy was like a vision of heaven...perfection, awesome, beautiful, serenity, laughter, peaceful, complete joy, and no regrets.

When my first granddaughter, Josefina, was born, I would make up songs in various tunes as I sang her to sleep. It worked every time. I could never sing the songs the same way I had previously, although I used similar tunes. As she got older, I would act out the songs I sang to her.

When Josefina learned to talk, I continued singing my made-up songs, and she continued to enjoy them. She and I laughed a lot as I sang and danced. I even taught Josefina her alphabets and how to spell her given name by using musical tunes as I acted out each letter with a different tune and facial expression. After a while, Josefina would repeat the alphabets and spell her name by herself. Later, Josefina told me that I had made learning fun from a very young age, and she remembered hearing my made-up songs and seeing my facial expressions with pleasure.

When Josefina was around three years old, I told her she could choose one treat for herself. Every time, she always chose two treats…one for John and one for herself. When Josefina's second brother, Josue, was born and could eat regular foods, Josefina always chose three treats…one for John, one for Josue, and one for herself.

Robert took note of Josefina's thoughtfulness and generosity and commented that he knew how I had been by observing Josefina's behavior. His comment touched my soul so profoundly that I cried tears of joy and hugged him at the same time. That was one of the few times I had been given credit for just being myself…the way God had created me. Words can heal long-ago wounds, and I placed Robert's words over all of my past wounds and scars and never looked back by focusing on Robert's words. I loved Robert deeply before he said those words, but somehow, my love deepened. It was God's goodness in Robert, the love of my life.

Although I had attempted to follow the tradition of sending cards to my family and friends on their special days, I was very inconsistent in that matter. However, I had my granddaughter, Josefina who never forgot her immediate family birthdays, anniversaries, Mother's Day, Father's Day, Thanksgiving, Christmas, any day of the week, etc., by sending each one of us personal cards. We could tell she had spent a lot of time reading and choosing each card before purchasing them. Josefina made me proud; words could never adequately express my pride and pleasure. And she did it out of love for all of us and not because it was a tradition.

When Josue was born, Robert and I had plenty of experiences as grandparents, and we had gotten used to our normal routines being disrupted. He was not very demanding, and as long as his diapers were changed regularly and he was fed on time, it was not complicated for us to provide care for him. We just ensured we had diapers, wipes, Vaseline, a variety of foods, etc., to meet his needs. His older siblings greatly influenced him, and he was smarter than they were at similar ages. It was pure joy taking care of Josue.

My heart went out to Josue, because I know how it felt to be in the middle of a large family and be one of the quieter ones. I felt that Josue was quieter, because his two older siblings were extroverts, and he was an introvert.

My fourth grandchild was given Daddy's namesake, Jacob. Angela's thoughtfulness in naming her third son after Daddy made up for all of the years, she had said that she hated me and everything about me. I knew that Angela had never actually hated me. Yet, I had been hurt by her words and actions. Every time I saw and thought of my grandson, Jacob, I had a smile on my face and wonderful feelings inward and outward. Jacob had an older spirit as if he had been born with wisdom beyond his years.

He reminded me of Daddy in many ways. The main difference between Daddy and Jacob was that Daddy was known for being very talkative. Jacob was on the quieter side unless he was asked questions. To my knowledge, Daddy was never in any physical fights, and Jacob did not engage in physical fights either. Jacob followed the rules even when bullies attacked him and reported the offenses to the proper adults. He made attempts to settle all disagreements with diplomacy.

When Robert Jr decided to marry, Robert and I were elated. We remembered when Robert Jr had invited us out to dinner so that we would meet his girlfriend. I was not excited about meeting another girlfriend of Robert Jr's, and I had told him many years earlier never to introduce me to his girlfriend unless he was going to marry her. My heart had been broken a couple of times in the past when Robert Jr and his girlfriends ended their relationship.

Therefore, I suggested to Robert that we dine at the Ninety-Nine Restaurant, because I was not attempting to impress Robert Jr or his new girlfriend. Within ten minutes or less after meeting Towana, I regretted my decision to dine at the Ninety-Nine Restaurant. I wondered if Robert felt the same way.

After dinner was over and as Robert and I were walking to our car, we both felt that we had chosen Towana for Robert, Jr., And we hoped that he would recognize Towana as his future wife. I expressed embarrassment for taking Towana to the Ninety-Nine Restaurant, because she was five-star material in my book, which meant Towana deserved the best in everything.

Later, I apologized face to face to Towana for my oversite and invited her to attend our traditional worship service at my church. I wanted Towana to know Robert and me better. I desired Towana to know that we were people of faith who attended church regularly; we were involved in the affairs in the community where our church was located, and we were spiritual people, not religious ones. By spiritual, I meant that we made efforts to love God first and best, to love ourselves, and to love others as we love ourselves...living God's Word rather than just telling them.

I remember the day of Robert Jr. and Tawana's wedding as if it were yesterday; it was 72 degrees and sunny. I felt as if God was smiling down on us; I felt God's presence in each of us, and God was speaking to all of us. All the guests expressed tears of joy and an atmosphere of gladness. Everyone spoke positive words to each other; there was a feeling of camaraderie and friendship, and they expressed their true feelings on Robert's wedding day, because the older adults had known him practically all of his natural life. I was elated that there were no spectators in attendance.

Robert and I became grandparents again to a new grandson, Robert Riley. Towana and Robert, Jr honored Robert with his namesake and honored Towana's father with her father's namesake. We were all very pleased, and he was adored by all four of us from the beginning of his life and remains so. I made a point to stop by Robert's and Towana's residence at every opportunity so that Robert Riley would grow up always knowing me and having fun with lots of laughter.

For the longest time, Robert Riley thought of me as his playmate, because we would run outside and climb the big tree in his parents' backyard. I made sure that I would be on the floor with him so that my head was as near to his head level as possible while visiting him. Even on Sundays, I had many experiences when Robert Riley burped up his mother's milk onto my Sunday dress clothes, and I never missed a beat. There was nothing that Robert Riley did that displeased me. I just took my soiled clothes to the dry cleaners.

Then, twenty months later, Robert, Jr., and Towana gave birth to my sixth grandchild and gave her their chosen name, with both of her maternal grandmothers' first names as her middle names. In that way, both of her grandmothers were honored. I was beside myself with gratitude to them. I acted the same way and did the same things I had done with Robert Riley, and Ariana has never known a day in her life that she did not know me.

As a matter of fact, I became a playmate to my grandchildren, Robert Riley and Ariana, and I continued to run around in the yard, play on the floor, and babysit them as often as I was asked. I even suggested that Robert, Jr., and Towana go out in the evenings and on Saturdays more so I could babysit both of them.

Being a grandmother has been much more enjoyable than being a mother. As a mother, I was responsible for being the best parent I could be. I was often burdened with those tremendous responsibilities, and I could not give up on myself by not trying to improve my parenting skills.

As a grandmother, I had fun and much more fun with all of my grandchildren. I've told them countless times how grateful I am to be their grandmother and that they are my grandchildren. And in my eyes, they are perfect. I've left all of their raising and discipline to their parents. God saved the best for the last for me…being a grandmother surpassed being a mother. Thank God!

Since my great-granddaughter doesn't live in the area of Massachusetts that I frequent on a regular basis, my visitations with her have been primarily scheduled from Fridays through Sundays. My granddaughter brings my great-granddaughter to my hotel room on Friday evenings and picks her up on Sundays before noon. In this way, I've had time to relax on Fridays after my long drive to the hotel before my great-granddaughter arrived at the hotel.

Our Friday nights have been filled with numerous table games, food, singing, and conversations. As a matter of fact, my great-granddaughter has never exhausted herself when she and I have been together. And the only way I have been able to get her to retire has been permitting her to watch a TV child's program on mute. I've been attempting to teach my great-granddaughter the principle that the early bird gets the worm. So far, it has not worked.

On Saturdays, our days have been full of shopping for books, building bear adventures, and playing in the parks. For two years now, the places we have gone have been selected very carefully because of the ongoing COVID-19 pandemic. I am eagerly looking forward to my great-granddaughter spending weekends and vacations with Robert and me. I remain very hopeful and excited about the prospects.

As the pandemic continues, my visitations have not been as frequent as I would have liked. I'm fortunate to get to see my great-granddaughter once each year. Therefore, I make the most of our visitations together and indulge her with everything she wants and many of the things I want her to have. God has blessed me with three generations of my descendants while I am still alive. Praise and thank God! And each generation has been included in my will. Proverbs 13:22 says a good person leaves an inheritance for their children's children, but a sinner's wealth is stored up for the righteous. Since I have a great-grandchild, I've included her in my will, along with my children and grandchildren.

7
My Musings

> I rise before dawn and cry for help; I have put my hope in your word.
>
> My eyes stay open through the watches of the night, that I may meditate on your promises (Psalm 119:147-149, NIV).

I don't believe or accept that I should selfishly keep the knowledge that could help someone else. Knowledge is powerful, and no human person possesses all the knowledge and experiences necessary to know everything. I'm sharing the knowledge and experiences I have acquired with others in hopes that they would avoid some situations and be better equipped to work through their difficult situations, circumstances, and events more successfully after reading about my experiences. Hopefully, just knowing that I have managed to live through my struggles and remained sane will be helpful to some folks.

As 2022 was ushered in, there has been a rapid surge in the omicron COVID-19 variant in people. Although fewer people were dying from the omicron variant, more children were being infected. I asked myself, but what about the children? All children are gifts from God, the Creator of us all, and should be treated as such by everyone.

Actually, do the majority of the adults in the United States and the world care about the welfare of children, or are they merely giving lip service to the health and welfare of children? Actions speak louder than words. Unfortunately, masses often rally around those people making the loudest noises. And oftentimes, those people making the loudest noises are not necessarily correct.

The vaccinated and boosted aren't the culprits in spreading COVID-19 and its variants. It's primarily a continuous pandemic, because the unvaccinated and unboosted people have failed to do their duty in protecting the children and others. COVID-19 and its variants will always cause breakthrough cases. Still, we would be able to co-exist with COVID-19 and its variants if at least eighty percent or more people in the United States consented to take the COVID-19 vaccination and booster shot.

Children rely on adults to protect them, and as an enlightened society, we have failed to be our sisters' and brothers' keepers. Proverbs 1:7 says the fear of the Lord is the beginning of knowledge, but fools despise wisdom and instruction (KJV).

My brain has been unable to comprehend the useless deaths of so many people in the United States and the world, because they refused to be vaccinated and boosted. I don't believe anyone should be forced to get vaccinated and boosted. However, I do believe that those unvaccinated and unboosted persons should love themselves and others enough to do no harm by practicing the reputable mitigations recommended by public health experts.

Every time I frequented the supermarkets, numerous individuals were unmasked, and many masked individuals had their masks covering only their mouths. All life should be valued, appreciated, and celebrated. Yet, it appears that we've gotten it backward as a people. Let's begin celebrating each other's life! Let's begin appreciating each other's life!

I have never been in favor of attending funerals. Culturally, the tradition has been to have funerals so relatives, friends, and others can say goodbye to the deceased. I've known instances when families have created huge debts for funerals. Why? Who were those families attempting to impress? I am sure those efforts were wasted on the dead. So why host elaborate funerals for the dead? To me, elaborate funerals are ludicrous and unnecessary to spend excessive money on the dead when countless people are suffering in life.

I've wondered if I ever attended a funeral when everyone who spoke at the funeral told the honest truth about the dead. How can a person be reconciled with the fact that the same police officers, elected officials, families, and people, in general, had nothing good and decent to say about the dead until she/he was in a coffin and on display in front of the church or funeral home? Why Lie? Well, I have left notarized instructions with Robert, Angela, Robert, Jr, and Josefina to cremate my body and not spend any unnecessary money in the process.

In other words, I've instructed them to perform this last task for me as cheaply as possible. They have been instructed that they don't have to impress anybody and ignore the gossipers and haters. Because if they loved me as they proclaimed, I would have known it as I lived on this side of heaven, and if they didn't, it's too late for me to have known. Either way, I pray that God's mercy helps me to crossover into eternity with God once I have taken my last breath on this side of heaven.

Am I the only one who questioned the way people act toward the dead? Oftentimes, as long as those same individuals were alive, they had been talked about, lied to, beaten down, disrespected, lacked support and encouragement in their times of need, incarcerated unjustly, unloved, sexually and physically molested, overlooked, etc.

And now, those same undervalued dead individuals have had elaborate funerals and were shown respect by the same people who had mistreated them. This tradition tops the oxymorons' list of all other oxymorons. Imagine the countless times we've seen the dead with police escorts, beginning at the churches or funeral homes all the way to the cemeteries and crematories. Oftentimes, I've been disgusted while witnessing such hypocritical acts the people demonstrated. Each time, I remained silent…to each their own. I have chosen to have my dead body cremated and not be on display for anyone except my husband, two children, grandchildren, and great-grandchildren, only if they desire to. Otherwise, I've given notarized instructions to make my cremation process as short and inexpensive as possible.

Why does bad news travel faster than good news? Back in the day, there were no social media such as Meta (formerly Facebook), Twitter, email, text, internet, TikTok, etc. Yet, people communicated with each other. Bad news traveled faster than good news, even back in the day. However, it took much longer to reach the masses of people with both bad and good news.

For example, in 1865, the enslaved African Americans in Alabama, the beautiful received the news that the Civil War had ended on May 28th. For the entire seventeen years, I lived in Alabama, the beautiful African Americans took May 28th off from work to celebrate our emancipation from industrialized slavery. It was a special day for us. In history classes, I learned that the last enslaved African American in Texas did not receive the news that the Civil War had ended until June 19th, and the Northern Union soldiers were victorious over the Southern Confederate soldiers. June 19th became known and celebrated as Juneteenth by African Americans annually.

When I was growing up in Alabama, the beautiful primary sources of communication besides face-to-face communication were telephones, telegrams, televisions, radios, newspapers, and magazines. There may have been other means, but they don't come to mind at the moment.

There have always been some people more morally and ethnically than others. Yet, there were certain behaviors that many individuals shared, even when they were churched or unchurched. I remember when people's houses burned down, people from all walks of life and ethnic groups came together to help the burned-out families. I was one of those children who wore my classmates' former dresses, sweaters, skirts, and blouses. I would not have known this information until some of them told others that I was wearing their former clothes. I was very embarrassed, but I sucked it up and never said anything to anyone of them.

Besides, I had nothing else to wear, and my parents needed the generosities of the people in the communities to help them get back on their feet after our house and its contents had burned. My siblings were in the same situation as I was. Some of my siblings fought the gossipers, but I never fought them. I did not desire to endure the consequences of fighting in public, because Mama's and Daddy's primary discipline for such a grave offense was whipping. So, I just kept quiet, although I didn't feel good about keeping quiet. In my mind, I knew it was a blessing to have clothes to wear.

When my parents' house burned down, I was very perplexed about the generosity of such diverse groups of people. I was not surprised that black folks came to our rescue, but I was very surprised at the generosity of the white folks.

You see, these were the same white folks who had called my family and I niggers all of my young life and had disrespected all of us, because we were black. Yet, when my family and I needed help, they readily donated toward fulfilling our needs. Mama and Daddy stood with broad smiles on their faces as they thanked each and every one of them. They were sincere because they were genuinely thankful that God had changed those white folks' hearts...even if it was only temporarily.

As I was approaching sixteen, I experienced another embarrassing situation. Some classmates came to my house before I finished my household chores. I don't know how the other homes looked early in the mornings. But my house was very messy by the end of each day. And so, I had to perform many household chores daily when I was not working in the fields to bring some form of order.

Frequently, I felt that as soon I had everything cleaned and everything was in its proper place, some of my younger siblings would mess things up again. By the time I retired every night, I was just too tired to start the process of cleaning all over again. I could barely finish washing all of the pots and pans. Early each morning, I would begin cleaning and straightening up the house.

On that particular morning, I had swept all the trash in one large pile. I was bending over to begin putting the trash in a trash bag when several of my classmates walked in. I felt my blood rushing to my face, because I was too embarrassed for them to see how much trash was on the floor. I knew it was from just one day. I remember thinking that they thought my house did not get cleaned regularly since that amount of trash would almost fill up a thirteen-gallon trash bag. It amazed me that a simple occurrence that happened when I was almost sixteen remains so vivid to me. I've had many embarrassing moments, some of which were worse than others.

Referring back to bad news traveling faster than good news, why is this so? I don't have all of the answers and reasons. I know that some people feel comfortable spreading more bad news than good news. Some believers in Jesus Christ even have difficulty sharing more good news than bad news. For example, four of us had dinner together, and I said that the deacons' scholarship ministry, which awards monetary scholarships to first-year college students, was an excellent ministry. Within less than sixty seconds, the other three believers quickly shared numerous complaints about the failure of many deacons not participating in their ministry. Go figure.

I have a fifteen-year-old grandson, and he's at the age of liking girls. He asked a particular girl if she would attend a special upcoming dance with him, and she agreed. In the meantime, my grandson asked his dad what type of clothing he should wear to the special dance and was told a suit would be most appropriate. My husband, son, and grandson made an adventure out of shopping for a suit and dress shoes for my grandson, which ended with a nice sit-down dinner.

A few days later, the girl my grandson, had asked to attend the special dance with him was sharing her feelings on social media and how awkward she felt when my grandson asked her to attend the special dance with him in the presence of other students. My grandson discovered that a good childhood friend was going around verbally bullying him about what the girl said on social media. My grandson was hurt and embarrassed about the entire scenario. So, he walked up to his childhood friend and punched him as hard as he could four times. My son was immediately summoned to his son's school to pick up his son. This incident happened a couple of days before Thanksgiving.

During the Thanksgiving break, my grandson lost many privileges as punishment for fighting in school. A mini trip to the Berkshires in western Massachusetts was canceled. Of course, my son and daughter-in-law were in distress over the entire situation.

Within twenty-four hours after the fight, my grandson asked his mom's permission to use his phone so he could call his childhood friend to apologize to him. My grandson's childhood friend told my grandson that he had been agonizing over how he could apologize to him and whether his actions had permanently jeopardized their friendship. He stated that he was unaware of the magnitude of the pain and embarrassment his actions had caused my grandson, and he regretted his actions. Both of them accepted each other's apology and remained good childhood friends. This scenario of bullying among friends ended well, but how many other teenagers know about it if my grandson and his childhood friend don't share the outcome of their confrontation in school? Well, I believe very few!

Why? Because good news travels slower than bad news. Most people enjoy sharing bad news with the masses. I suggested to my son that there was a higher purpose to be achieved than merely two childhood friends admitting their errors, apologizing, and continuing to be good childhood friends. I said, "This true story should be shared with as many teenagers as possible through social media about all kinds of bullying and the harmful effects of bullying. Even social bullying among good childhood friends caused physical fistfights in their schools. The two young teenagers could keep their identities unanimously as they shared their stories. I explained to my son that if I shared this story with teenagers, it would not have the same effect.

As our conversation continued, Robert Jr gave several reasons why he was unsure about my suggestion. I was not suggesting that he act on my suggestion immediately but that he should take the time to pray and think about it. And not rush into anything. But allow the Holy Spirit to instruct and guide him in his decisions. I believe daily that millions of good things are happening among teenagers that are not shared through social media, and they should be. I believe there is more good news than bad news, but people are hesitant to share the frequent occurrence of good news with others, especially on social media. Therefore, teenagers and children just do what the adults do and follow their examples as if it's a badge of honor.

Someone needs to start from somewhere. Why not start with these two childhood good friends? Greta Thunberg began with a movement of one...herself, and now, politicians, CEOs, private companies, etc., throughout the world are being held accountable for climate change.

These two childhood friends could start a movement against all kinds of bullying by sharing their stories with the massive teenage populations throughout the world. Think about it. If bullying resulted in two childhood friends fighting in school, what about the harm bullying has caused and is causing to those teenagers who don't have any friendships with the bullies? Bullying is a pandemic and public health problem. All of us should be concerned and do our best at all opportunities to help end bullying forever.

Oftentimes, I have felt out of step with the people around me. It was as if they and I were marching to very different rhythms of life. And because they and I have very rarely been in step or beat with each other, true friendships never materialized between us. Many have claimed to be my friend. Yet, over time, I discovered they were not. At least they were not my true friends but fake friends.

Psalm 55:21 says their talk is smooth as butter, yet war is in their heart; their words are more soothing than oil, yet they are drawn swords (NIV, paraphrased), and Psalm 12:2 says everyone lies to their neighbor; they flatter with their lips but harbor deception in their hearts (NIV).

During one of many mundane and very challenging periods of my life, God gave me a fifteen-year-old daughter who accepted me just the way I was. God knew exactly what I needed even before I knew. I needed Genesi in my life. I count her being my daughter and being part of my life as pure joy. She continues to have my unconditional love, and Genesi will remain in my prayers, thoughts, and heart.

Those years with Genesi's presence remind me of the passage of Scripture in James 1:2-4 that says to consider it pure joy, Margaret, whenever I face trials of many kinds because I know that the testing of my faith develops perseverance. Perseverance must finish its work so that I may be mature (NIV, personalized).

As time passes, I appreciate and continue to keep my true friends close to me and in my prayers, thoughts, and heart. Reflecting over my life, I've had numerous shared interactions and experiences with individuals from all walks of life. Because most of the people I have known and worked with on numerous issues and traveled in different circles, I've managed to avoid confusing my professional, business, political, etc. relationships with my personal life and true friendships. I have spent countless hours with different individuals through the years working on social justice issues through the brainstorming and implementation phases, participating and attending community events, and participating and attending professional events without considering my financial losses and the amount of time those relationships required of me. The more involved I got, the more time I committed to those endeavors.

Yet, my true friends never complained to me that I don't spend enough time with them to help nurture our friendships. Even after months had passed and we finally met up, it was as if we had just talked to each other the day before. There were never any accusatory conversations about me neglecting our friendship. We were just happy and pleased to be in each other's presence.

Three of my true friends and I belong to the same church, and we met each other as we attended church worship services at church and community events. Just from the fact that the three of us have shared many commonalities, we are also very different in many ways. We were raised in large families; we were raised in the South, and we have been in committed relationships with our husbands for several decades. In fact, our differences have made our total relationship with each other richer. By the way, the four of us are black.

My fourth true friend and I are of different races. She and I belong to different churches; we share similar upbringings; although she was born and raised in the Northeast, and I was born and raised in the South, we have generously shared our similarities, appreciated our differences, and celebrated our humanity together.

One of my true friends has defended me and my honor against anyone and everybody. She has given me credit where credit has been due, and she has never stopped doing this, whether in meetings or in the public arenas. And she has never told me that she has done this. The best pastor I have ever had on this side of heaven informed me of this fact many years ago. By the way, she is an excellent cook, and her house remains the cleanest house I have had the privilege of entering. This true friend and I share similar values in regard to germs, viruses, bacteria, etc. We are highly committed germophobes!

Another true friend recognized that God had called me to professional ministry; she told me face to face that God had called me to preach and teach the gospel of Jesus Christ while we were on a couples' camping trip in upstate New York, and she patiently waited for me to publicly acknowledge God's call without ever mentioning our initial conversation again.

My other true friend and her husband have traveled extensively with my husband and me over the years and shared countless lengthy face-to-face and phone conversations with each other. She has been the only person other than my family members who has shared lengthy phone conversations with me. I've never permitted the telephone to be the main line of communication in my personal life since I am and always have been a face-to-face communicator.

My fourth true friend and I met while we taught at Tufts University School of Dental Medicine (TUSDM). I had been teaching at TUSDM for at least ten to twelve years when she began teaching there. Our teaching schedule overlapped only one day per week, and we found ourselves very excited to have the opportunity to interact with each other on that one day a week.

Over the years, we have shared her youngest son's wedding together; we have had many husbands' and wives' dinners and lunches together, and she and her husband have supported me in my professional ministry journey by being faithful cheerleaders on some occasions when I have been scheduled to preach.

Even though she and her husband relocated to Michigan for a couple of years, my true friend contacted me as soon as she arrived back in Massachusetts. Now that she and her husband have relocated to Texas, we share text messages with each other. There may be a slim chance that we never meet face to face again on this side of heaven. Yet, our genuine friendship will last; one day, we will meet in eternity.

As I recognized decades ago, one must spend time with those individuals outside of organized events and functions to develop genuine relationships with individuals. My four true friends and I have been involved with each other in our personal lives, such as attending my annual family unions in my birth state, sharing foods in our homes, attending family cookouts, dining out in different restaurants, vacationing together, playing table games in each other homes, etc. Our friendships developed into genuine relationships because we have spent time with each other beyond attending Bible study, church worship services, church meetings, and events together.

Regardless of the toxic environment in God's world, all four of my true friends and I have faith in God, and we live by our faith in God and not by sight. We treasure family and friendships and appreciate each other just as we are. Neither of us has desired or attempted to make clones of ourselves. We have accepted our authentic selves and appreciate and celebrate our authentic relationships in love…God's love for us and our love for each other.

Everybody cannot be a theologian. Everybody cannot be a Martin Luther, Malcolm X, Shirley Chisolm, former president Barrack Obama, vice-president Kamal Harris, Amanda Gorman, Greta Thunberg, Stephen Curry, Rev. Dr. Martin

Luther King, Dr. Kizzmekia Corbert, Alice Walker, etc. Yet, all of us can become the best version of ourselves with willing minds because we all have an able God! With God's help, I am committed to continuing to become the best version of myself. And I am praying for others to become the best versions of themselves.

Psalm 23 says the Lord is my shepherd. I shall lack nothing. The Lord makes me lie down in green pastures, the Lord leads me besides quiet waters, the Lord restores my soul. The Lord guides me in the paths of righteousness for the Lord's namesake. Even though I walk through the valley of death, I fear no evil, for the Lord is with me. The Lord's rod and the Lord's staff, they comfort me. The Lord prepares a table before me in the presence of my enemies. The Lord anoints my head with oil; my cup overflows. Surely goodness and love will follow me all the days of my life, and I will dwell in the house of the Lord forever (NIV, personalized). Thank you, God!

Oftentimes, I have wondered why some people die at very young ages. I remember when I was fourteen years old, and I prayed to God to allow me to live until at least the year 2000. When I was fourteen, I thought to be fifty-three years old in the year 2000 would be very old. I am so grateful to God that God had other plans for me. When I turned fifty-three, I did not feel or look old after thirty-nine years later; I still don't feel old, and I just look older. Some people have lived much shorter lives than others and have greatly pleased God in their brief lives. I believe God has much more work for me to to help build up God's kingdom, even in my golden years.

There are many Scriptures on living a long life. God desires that I don't waste my life on useless things and tasks.

Just as Proverbs 16:31 says gray hair is a crown of splendor; it is attained by a righteous life (NIV), and Ephesians 6:2-3 says “honor my father and mother”- which is the first commandment with a promise – “that it will go well with me and that I may enjoy long life on earth (NIV, personalized), God has given me a long life which is much longer than I prayed for at the age of fourteen.

There is good in everybody. One has to search a little deeper to connect with the good in some individuals. Investing time in ourselves and people is never wasted, and investing time and money on children are always beneficial. My suggestion to everyone is quietness…frequent moments of quietness. God has frequently spoken to me in quietness, and when God spoke to me in quietness, there was no doubt that it was God’s voice I heard. God gave me one life to live out on this side of heaven, and I have tried my best to make the best of it. I am still trying.

I have lived much longer with God being the head of my life than without attempting to please God in every area of my life. Death and I remain strangers to each other, and I have no desire to become a friend of death at this juncture of my life. Death and I remain just like oil and water and day and night. Oil and water don’t mix well; day and night are polar opposites.

Literally, I do not function well in darkness. Death reminds me of being in pitch-black darkness without the presence of God! And God is alive! God is not dead! I am alive and breathing the holy breath, God gave me. I know it is inevitable that death and I will meet face to face in order for me to meet God in eternity.

In the meantime, I am grateful to God for life, freedom, health, and all of the countless blessings from God with my name attached to them. My life is in God's care! Psalm 121: 1-8 says I lift up my eyes to the hills, where does my help come from? My help comes from the Lord, the Maker of heaven and earth. The Lord will not let my foot slip, the Lord who watches over me will neither slumber nor sleep. The Lord watches over me. The Lord is my shade at my right hand; the sun will not harm me by day, nor the moon by night. The Lord will keep me from harm. The Lord will watch over my coming and my going both now and forevermore (NIV, personalized).

Has anyone pondered the fact that God always knew how each of our lives would turn out? I don't believe I am the only one. God knew and has always known the right and wrong decisions we would make and the right and wrong acts we would commit, even before birth. Our prophetic God gives us plenty of opportunities to do the right thing. It's not like we don't have time to change our minds. It's just that God already knows the outcome of the when, where, what, and how of our thoughts, decisions, deeds, omissions, etc. The fact about Judas' betrayal used to confuse me profoundly, and the Scriptures that clarified this fact to me were Psalm 109:8 and Mark 14:44-46.

It has taken me many years of prayer, studying the Bible, meditation, asking God questions, frequent periods of quietness, etc., to understand what these two Scriptures meant finally. God already knew Judas was going through with his betrayal of Jesus for thirty pieces of silver coins, although God gave him plenty of opportunities to change his mind. This was an example of the prophetic Word of God! In this same way, we have opportunities to do what's right, although God already knows each of our outcomes.

Whenever someone says I couldn't help myself, I know they lied. All of us can help ourselves, because God has already given us that ability. Thank God!

During one of my meetings with Pastor Walker, he told me that he knew I had the gift of prophecy…things that were forthcoming. I knew it and never told him or anyone. Actually, I wondered what purpose the Holy Spirit gifted me with the gift of prophecy, just as I questioned God why God called me to preach and teach the gospel of Jesus Christ. I had surmised that I should not do something until I have instructions and guidance from the Holy Spirit, and being called to professional ministry and possessing the gift of prophecy were two of them.

As I was vacationing in upstate New York, the evening news showed Princess Diana and her new manfriend being hounded by numerous paparazzi with their cameras. It had been reported that the two of them sunbathed in the nude on the rooftop where they were staying. I thought to myself Princess Diana and her manfriend should be left alone. They deserved some privacy, just as everyone else. So, why make such a big deal over them sunbathing in the nude on a rooftop? As I went outside, I wondered how the people would react if Princess Diana died. The following week, Princess Diana died in a car accident. I was astounded when I heard the breaking news about her death. I only shared my previous thoughts about wondering how people would behave over Princess Diana's death with one person until now.

In 2002, I was returning home from visiting my siblings, and as I was riding the Logan Express bus from Boston Logan

International Airport en route to Braintree, Massachusetts, I observed a very high and large embankment to my left, which was part of the support structure of the highway. I wondered what would happen if that support structure crumbled as I continued staring at the embankment for a few more seconds. Lo and behold, a bridge collapsed in Oklahoma on Interstate 40 a few days later. I had mentioned my thoughts about a bridge collapse to only one other person until now.

In reflection, I don't recall any other tragedies I had thought about before those two tragedies happened. In other words, my mind had not conceived of any tragic event beforehand until then. I wondered why God had shown me those two tragedies in advance. And I have wondered and asked God why those two tragedies.

It had taken me twenty-four years to publicly reveal that God had called me to preach and teach the gospel of Jesus Christ to Pastor Walker. And it was not until after the second tragedy had been revealed to me beforehand and then happened that I embraced the fact that the Holy Spirit had given me the gift of prophecy. Henceforth, I stopped denying God's call on my life and the gift of prophecy.

Over the years, with the power of the Holy Spirit, I knew my church would endure many years of turmoil. Initially, the type of turmoil my church would experience was unclear. Yet, I was confident that it would happen, and it did. We are still going through the turmoil of spiritual warfare at my church. Many members who were the culprits in the ongoing spiritual warfare are dead, and many remain on this side of heaven. Many Scriptures have helped my endurance, and the following Scriptures are some of them in personalized versions.

How can I keep my way pure? By living according to God's Word, I seek God with all my heart; do not let me stray from God's commands, I have hidden God's Word in my heart that I might not sin against God (Psalm 119:9-11, NIV, personalized).

Trust in the Lord and do good; dwell in the land and enjoy safe pasture. Delight myself in the Lord and the Lord will give me the desires of my heart, commit my way to the Lord: trust in the Lord and the Lord will do this: The Lord will make my righteousness shine like the dawn, the justice of my cause like the noonday sun (Psalm 37:3-6, NIV, personalized).

For God knows the plans God has for me, plans to prosper me and not harm me, plans to give me hope and a future (Jeremiah 29:11, NIV, personalized).

And I know that in all things God works for the good of Margaret who loves God, who has been called according to God's purpose (Romans 8:28, NIV, personalized).

For God so loved me that God gave God's one and only Son, if I believe in Jesus, I shall not perish but have eternal life (John 3:16, NIV, personalized).

If I have any encouragement from being united with Christ, if any comfort from Christ's love, if any fellowship with the Spirit, if any tenderness and compassion, then make my joy complete by being like-minded, having the same love, being one in spirit and purpose. Do nothing out of selfish ambition or vain conceit, but in humility, consider others better than myself. I should look not only to my own interests but also to the interests of others. My attitude should be the same as that of Christ Jesus: Who being in very nature God, did not consider equality with God something to be grasped, but made himself nothing, taking the very nature of a servant, being made in human likeness. And being found in appearance as a man, Jesus humbled himself and became obedient to death – even death on a cross. Therefore, God exalted Jesus to the highest place and gave him the name that is above every name, that at the name Jesus every name knee should bow, in heaven and on earth and under the earth, and every tongue confess that Jesus Christ is Lord. To the glory of God, the Father (Philippians 2:1-10, NIV, personalized).

The forces of evil are real, and we are facing a moral crisis at the highest levels in God's world. According to numerous people, there had been a general belief that the ideals of democracy for all Americans were worthy of striving for across political, social, educational, and economic lines.

Since all of us are God's people, my brain cannot understand the fact that there are people who justify that all people qualified and registered to vote should not have their God-given right to vote in all local, state, and national elections, especially the believers in Jesus Christ. Don't they know that God shows no favoritism among people? It's people who establish invisible walls in the form of unjust systems in all areas of the private sectors, banking, educational, local, state, and federal institutions against people, resulting in disparities among the masses.

I have learned through studying the Bible, meditation, prayer, attending worship services, retreats, Christian workshops, lectures, etc., that all of us will have zero balances here on earth when we die. There won't be any outstanding debts for any of us. None of us, with faith in God, has gotten everything right. In the sight of God, it does not matter whether believers are world-renowned, unknown, or average. God is an inclusive God, and some people are not applying inclusivity in their daily lives (referencing Luke 16:19-36, ESV). Yet, we should keep trying daily to improve once we know better. So, stop making excuses and learn from the Biblical story of Genesis 3.

Oftentimes, democrats, republicans, and independents tossed aside their personal differences and worked together to preserve and protect those ideals of democracy. I am in agreement with those persons who said although the ideals of democracy have never been obtained and lived out in our society, this does not mean we, as a people, should not continue to be examples of being good Samaritans as the gospels of Matthew, Mark, Luke, and John exemplified in their narratives.

Therefore, I am in total agreement with those persons who promote the ideals of democracy and have committed themselves to the general good of the masses. We, the people of the United States of America, should be proud to be Americans and commit ourselves to preserving every fabric of the ideals of democracy and keeping hope alive for each generation of people.

Only through the grace of God can Robert and I persevere through many challenging years and remain happily married to each other. I can honestly say that I am truly grateful that Robert and I worked through all of our difficulties…it has been worth it.

Being alive long enough to grow old continues to be a blessing from God. Truthfully, I would choose the last four years if it were possible to relive any of my life over again.

Although, the people of the world continued to promote evil of all kinds. The peace of God that transcends all of my understanding has been inside of me...my mind, thoughts, heart, and dreams. I know that God has helped me to walk by faith and not by sight and kept me uplifted as I have lived each day through the ongoing pandemic. Although I have not seen COVID-19 and its variants and have no idea where they could be found, God has always known. And God provided instructions for me to listen, learn, and follow through reputable public health experts.

As I continue to enjoy each day to the fullest, I have made concerted efforts to keep everything revealed in this book accurate, and God continues to save the best part of my life for the last!

The joys of being the mother of two healthy and successful adult children are indescribable. I eagerly look forward to sending out texts in the form of morning greetings and reading their responses. The sagas of Angela's and Robert Jr's teenage years adventures are continuously revealed to me as the days, weeks, and months pass. If I had known my children were being mischievous when they were teenagers, I probably would have been a nervous wreck and resorted to being constantly sedated for my nerves and anxieties.

As it turned out, I was spared knowing about their numerous disobedient occurrences. Just knowing about the ones Angela and Robert Jr committed was bad enough. Now, I laugh until my eyes tear up as they tell me of their unsupervised adventures. It's a wonderful feeling to laugh with them as they reveal those secrets of theirs, they have kept for me for decades. I am so grateful to God that God took good care of them during those times, and I wholeheartedly acknowledge that it was God's unconditional love for them. I don't attempt to get any of the credit, and even if I tried, it's useless...a complete waste of time.

There is a song that comes to my mind that says to count my blessings and name them one by one. Count my blessings, and see what God has done. When I think about the goodness of the Lord, my cup overflows. Being a grandmother of six grandchildren and great-grandmother of two great-grandchildren caused me to feel as if my cup had become larger than the Gulf of Mexico. I count it all pure joy: joy in the morning, joy in the noonday, joy at night, and joy 24/7.

The longer I live, the more I desire to be in God's presence to please God. There is a familiar passage of Scripture that has given me comfort and assurance of God's love for me that says for I am persuaded, that neither death, nor life, nor angels, nor principalities, nor powers, nor things present, nor things to come, nor height, nor depth, nor any other creature, shall be able to separate me from the love of God, which is in Christ Jesus my Lord (Romans 8:38-39, NIV, personalized).

Some people may think that my greatest accomplishments should be the five college degrees and the certificate in ministry I've earned through my tireless efforts and hard work. I do not make light of my educational and professional accomplishments, and I am very grateful that God had a better life waiting for me beyond my life in Alabama, the beautiful and sweet home of Alabama. Therefore, I firmly refute the opinions of others in this matter.

Clearly, I don't have all of the answers to my questions and other things. I don't even know why some people are born with disabilities, serious medical conditions, poverty, etc., and others are born with all of the advantages offered in life. Yet, God never overlooks any of God's people. Although, I do understand that God uses people as vessels to do the work to accomplish God's will, and there are numerous Scriptures throughout the Bible pertaining to the work of God being accomplished through the people of God.

As I continue to live on this side of heaven, I am still praying to the Holy Spirit for guidance and instructions. I still desire to please God and not people each day. God has never failed me yet, and God never will, because I know for myself that in all things God works for my good who loves God who has been called according to God's purpose (Romans 8:28, NIV, personalized).

Life is too precious of a gift from God to waste, and my greatest accomplishments in life are my two biological children, six grandchildren, and two great-grandchildren. In fact, I have been blessed with another great grandchild…a great grandson. Praise and thank God! Just as my parents', grandparents', and ancestors' spirits live on through me, my spirit and all of my ancestors' spirits will live on through my descendants. I believe memories about me will be talked about in positive ways, written about, appreciated, and celebrated for many generations to come, because I believe I've accomplished some positive things in my life that pleased God. I just simply believe! Glory to God!

9 798893 959482

Printed by Libri Plureos GmbH in Hamburg,
Germany